# WALKING IN LANCASHIRE

## ABOUT THE AUTHOR

'Every year hundreds of walkers place themselves in the hands of Mary Welsh. Meet her and it isn't hard to see why,' says *Cumbria Life* magazine. 'A 60-something, she's enthusiastic, imperturbable and, above all, considerate – someone you would happily rely on.' Mary is a travel writer and an award-winning writer of walking books, having produced more than 35 walking guidebooks. She writes regular columns in magazines and newspapers and for the internet.

She has lived in the north of England for nearly 30 years, after a childhood spent in rural Hertfordshire where she was educated and after which she went on to take a biology degree in London. Lancashire has provided her with some magnificent countryside and wonderful hidden corners to enjoy, where the noise of modern-day life does not impinge, and she hopes that you too will appreciate its many unexpected pleasures.

# WALKING IN LANCASHIRE

by
Mary Welsh

2 POLICE SQUARE, MILNTHORPE, CUMBRIA LA7 7PY
www.cicerone.co.uk

A catalogue record for this book is available from the British Library

Photos by the author

**OS** Ordnance Survey® This product includes mapping data licensed from Ordnance Survey® with the permission of the Controller of Her Majesty's Stationery Office. © Crown copyright 2003. All rights reserved. Licence number PU100012932

## Acknowledgements
My grateful thanks go to my four friends – Chris, Dora, Jane and Sue – who walked with me as I retraced my steps of 1996, the year of the first edition of this book. Generally the weather was good, but on some days it rained non-stop – and not one of them complained. Special thanks go to Jane, in particular, who kept the home ticking over when I was away for some very long days. Last but not least to Tom, my husband, for his unfailing support and advice.

*Mary Welsh*

*Front cover:* Nick's Chair, Blindhurst Fell

# CONTENTS

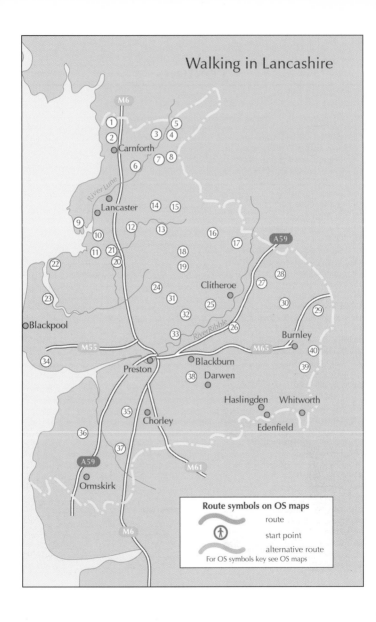

# Walking in Lancashire

# PREFACE

Lancashire, a county in the northwest of England, has a great variety of landscape. It is often thought of as an area of industrial towns, but these are to be found in a cluster towards its southern end. To the north, east and west and in the central part there is splendid walking country, and even between the large towns vast stretches of lonely moorland tempt walkers onto their heights.

Lancashire does not have mountains such as those known as Munros or Corbetts, but it does have some high hills. They include Weets Hill, the heights above Darwen, the Bleasdale Fells, Pendle Hill, Thieveley Pike, Longridge Fell, Clougha Pike and Ward's Stone, all of which tempt the walker to climb onto their long grassy ridges, from which there are panoramic views. Many of these are topped with sweet-smelling heather and some consist of peaty moorland where, generally, there is a path to help you along.

The county has a wealth of pretty villages, such as Arkholme, Nether Burrow, Chipping, Slaidburn, Ribchester, Bolton-by-Bowland, Downham and Croston, where you will want to linger. Try the walks in this book that either start in one of these villages, or pass through them.

*Stile onto Grit Fell (Walk 14)*

*Red roses on the waterboard bridge over the River Lune (Walk 5)*

Some of the walks take you beside Lancashire's wonderful rivers, including the stately Lune, where salmon jump and sand martins tunnel into the banks to nest. Or you can seek out the delights of the Marshaw Wyre and the Tarnbrook Wyre, which unite to form the River Wyre below Abbeystead Reservoir. Another trio of fine rivers, the Ribble, the Hodder and the Calder, can be enjoyed on one of the walks.

Deciduous woodlands, beautiful in bluebell time, abound. Try walking in late April and early May to see carpets of these lovely flowers in Grize Dale, and in the woods near Aughton where they border the River Lune.

Those who prefer breezy coastal rambles will enjoy a bracing walk from Cockerham along the Cocker Channel, or a stroll on the embankment that edges part of Morecambe Bay on your

return to Knott End, or a blustery walk round Sunderland Point – if the tide is right.

Lancashire offers a wealth of historic sites. The extensive ruins of Whalley Abbey can be visited at the beginning or end of a walk from Whalley itself. The bridges at Wycoller have to be seen to appreciate the workmanship of the builders – and from this lovely corner of the county there is a fine walk up onto the heights as well. Other bridges to be visited are Fairy Bridge near Downham, Cromwell's Bridge not far from Stonyhurst College and the Devil's Bridge at Kirkby Lonsdale.

If level ground is your choice for walking Lancashire can fulfil this desire too. The Lancaster Canal provides great towpath walks, where you are often rewarded with a flash of petrol blue as

Portal to what was once the harbour master's house – Sunderland (Walk 9)

a kingfisher flies low over the cut, perhaps at Glasson or Garstang. Or walk over the flat pastures between Martin Mere Wildfowl Centre and Mere Sands Wood Nature Reserve.

But a word of caution: on walks over remote fells, through lonely valleys or along quiet shores the effects of weather changes should not be underestimated. Go prepared with waterproofs, wear walking boots, take the maps you need and a compass – and be able to use it.

The relevant Ordnance Survey Explorer map is listed for each walk, and the maps shown in the book are from the Landranger series, 1:50,000 scale.

All the walks start from car parks or recognised parking areas and the relevant grid references are given. Many starting points are approached along narrow, quiet lanes where care should be taken in case you meet a farm vehicle or a flock of sheep. These lanes can be accessed from the M6, a tiresome motorway but one that is very useful for taking walkers close to the area to be walked.

The walks (all circular except one) range in length from 8 to 19km (5 to 12 miles) and all are suitable for most walkers. Some are gentle strolls that make a good introduction to the wonderful recreation of walking and help the less fit to prepare for more challenging walks.

Good walking!

*Mary Welsh*

## THE COUNTRY CODE

Remember that the countryside needs your care and respect – follow the Country Code.

1 Enjoy the countryside and respect its life and work.
2 Guard against all risk of fire.
3 Fasten all gates.
4 Keep dogs under close control.
5 Keep to public paths across farmland.
6 Use gates and stiles to cross hedges and walls.
7 Leave livestock, crops and machinery alone.
8 Take litter home.
9 Help to keep all water clean.
10 Protect wildlife, plants and trees.
11 Take special care on country roads.
12 Make no unnecessary noise.

# WALK 1

## *Silverdale*

| | |
|---|---|
| **Distance** | 10.5km (6½ miles) |
| **Time** | 3–4 hours |
| **Terrain** | Generally easy walking; walking boots advisable |
| **Maps** | OS Explorer OL7 |

The villages of Silverdale, Arnside and Storth border the estuary where the River Kent empties its waters into Morecambe Bay. Silvery limestone hills, where the pavement has been eroded into clints and grykes, erupt from the gentle pastures beyond the villages and give Silverdale its name. Many of the hills are skirted with deciduous woodlands, such as quaintly named Eaves, Gait Barrows, Cringlebarrow, Middlebarrow, Bottoms and Underlaid. Parts of Eaves Wood, where this walk starts, have been a broad-leaved woodland continuously since the 1600s.

Park in the easy-to-miss car park on the edge of Eaves Wood, Silverdale, grid ref 472759 (northwest of Leighton Moss visitor centre). Leave from the back of the parking area by a wide track beyond a gate to walk through ash, hazel, small-leaved lime and oak woodland. At the waymarked T-junction turn left to continue a short way along the edge of the wood to a Y-junction, where you begin to climb the right branch. Ascend steadily and at the next Y-junction take the right fork again. Follow the track as it begins to wind left, then at the first waymark you spot bear right to climb a wide track which is soon edged with limestone clints, and then becomes stepped. Emerge into an open area with limestone scarp to the right and go on past some crag-fast yew. Continue on until you reach a waymark directing you left for a short ascent onto a fine hillock. Ahead stands the Pepperpot, a

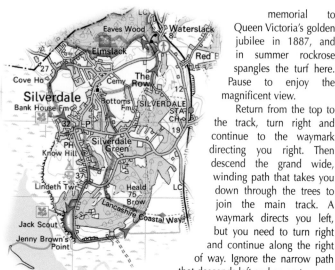

memorial to Queen Victoria's golden jubilee in 1887, and in summer rockrose spangles the turf here. Pause to enjoy the magnificent view.

Return from the top to the track, turn right and continue to the waymark directing you right. Then descend the grand wide, winding path that takes you down through the trees to join the main track. A waymark directs you left, but you need to turn right and continue along the right of way. Ignore the narrow path that descends left and go on to come beside a high stone wall on your left and two huge old water-storage troughs on your right. Carry on along the track to arrive at the narrow lane at Elmslack.

Cross the road and walk down signposted Cove Road. Watch out for arrows directing you down a continuing narrow walled-and-hedged way (Walling Lane) to pass below a house. Go through a gate to join a road, go ahead for a few steps, and where the road turns left take the walled track ahead to arrive at the road to Arnside.

Turn right and walk on. Cross as soon as possible and continue to where the busy road bends sharply right. Here turn left, signposted 'Cul-de-sac and to the shore'. This quickly brings you to a delightful cove with an intriguing cave to the right and a fine view of the bay. Then take the white kissing gate on the left and, beyond, climb a rising walled track with more fine views out to sea.

At the end of the track go through another kissing gate and follow the grassy trod across some gated pastures (the Lots) to join the road to Silverdale. Turn left and follow the road as it winds right. Where the main road swings left, cross with care and continue ahead up Stankelt Road, with the wall on your right, to take a signposted footpath on the right to Woodwell. Keep walking ahead on this quiet way, not deviating, and following the 'wriggle' in the path where it bends left and then goes on to the right. Carry on along the waymarked route until you join the road to Silverdale once more.

Turn right and at the T-junction walk left. Where this road swings left, go ahead down a 'No through road' to pass Lindeth Tower, where the writer Elizabeth Gaskell

*The Pepperpot, a memorial to Queen Victoria's golden jubilee*

The restored limekiln at Jack Scout

and her daughters stayed. From their sitting room at the top they watched travellers crossing the sands. Walk on to take a gate on the right into Jack Scout, a wonderful limestone promontory in the care of the National Trust. Pass the huge restored limekiln and continue ahead through the oak and hawthorn woodland to come to a path on the edge of the cliffs overlooking a great expanse of Morecambe Bay. Walk left until you can take a gate onto a minor road.

From here look out to sea for a dramatic view (tide permitting) of Jenny Brown's Point, a line of shingle-clad boulders stretching for nearly 1.6km (1 mile) towards the horizon. This was part of a scheme in the 19th century to reclaim Silverdale Sands. The House of Commons approved the scheme, but when the House of Lords did not agree the plan was abandoned and the line of boulders left to the birds.

Descend to end of the road and go on along the rough shore to wind round the outside of the wall in front of Brown's Houses, where Jenny lived. Continue on an easier way now, just above the shore, to pass a tall chimney (restored), once a limekiln, and then over sea-washed turf. Climb a stile and a short distance along take a rising path continuing just above a wet part of the route to come to a signpost. Here turn left to climb steepishly towards Heald Brow. Follow the waymarked path as it winds left and then right and crosses a stile into Heald Brow woodland, continuing through the trees to come to a stone stepped stile. Keep ahead with the wall to your left and wriggle through a gap beside a gate at the next wall. Carry on over the next stile into a clump of woodland then take a wicket gate to walk a track, right, to a road.

Cross the road and after a few steps right take a foot-path to Silverdale village. Drop down some steps then take the upper of two paths to walk along the 'cliffs'. Take care as you go along the top of the limestone scar and through the woodland, because for a short distance the land to your left drops steeply (children should be under control). When your reach an open area go ahead and climb a grassy slope into a wide area of grass. Turn left here and walk to a stile leading into more woodland. Carry on along the pleasing way until the path winds right, between a hedge on the left and a fenced pasture on the right, to come to a road.

Turn right and a short distance along cross and take the signed track 'To the church' going off left. Once through a gate take the grassy trod that runs beside a pasture with the walled gardens of houses to your left. Carry on beside the wall and follow it as it veers left and enters a small copse. Go through a gate and walk left to take a signposted right turn taking you in front of several bungalows and then out into a pasture. Halfway along take the white kissing gate in the wall on your left and continue along on the other side of the wall. Keep going until you come to a gate giving onto a road.

Turn right and after 50 metres take a signposted kissing gate where you walk on with the wall on your right. Go through the stile in the wall, on to the next white kissing gate, and then carry on ahead to a gate to a road called The Row. Turn left and walk along this quiet lane to its end. Cross with care to rejoin your car in the car park opposite.

# WALK 2

## *Warton Crag and Leighton Moss*

| | |
|---|---|
| **Distance** | 11.4km (7 miles) |
| **Time** | 4 hours |
| **Terrain** | Steady climb with some scrambling to trig point; generally good walking on grass, woodland paths and tracks, with some road walking |
| **Maps** | OS Explorer OL7 |

Start from the spacious quarry car park in Crag Road, just west of Warton village, grid ref 492724. From the

The original beacon on Warton Crag announced the sighting of the Spanish Armada in 1588. Pause on the summit and visualise the approach of the ships as you look out over Morecambe Bay. Leighton Hall is owned by Major and Mrs Gillow Reynolds, descendants of the famous Lancaster furniture makers Gillow & Co. In 1763 George Towneley had the house rebuilt in the Adam style, and the park laid out and the woods replanted. Beyond lies Leighton Moss Nature Reserve, its limestone floor covered with marine clay overlaid with peat. Water from the surrounding hills drains into the valley and forms three main meres. Around these grow extensive reed beds which have to be controlled to prevent them encroaching upon the open water.

This walk takes you first into Warton Crag Nature Reserve, then high over the crag itself before descending through fine deciduous woodland to edge marshland and then into Leighton Moss Nature Reserve. You then come close to Leighton Hall and over its gracious parkland, finally returning through Warton Crag Nature Reserve once more.

entrance take a footpath heading south in the direction of Warton. Continue through birch woodland, with Carnforth seen over the flat land to your right, and go down steps to a kissing gate into Warton Crag Nature

*Leighton Hall and Leighton Moss*

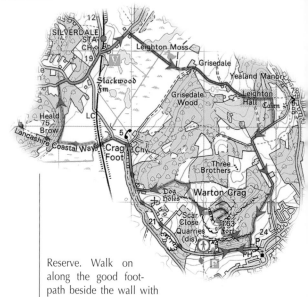

Reserve. Walk on
along the good foot-
path beside the wall with
the road to your right. At a signposted way turn left to
climb a short slope through trees, keeping parallel with
the wall to your right.

Ignoring the gap stile on the right, pass a nature-
reserve board and turn left up a well-trodden way marked
by a boulder in the centre of the path. Continue upwards
on a limestone terrace, moving up to a parallel terrace at
an easy pace. Repeat this again and go on to a stile in the
fence, which you climb – high above the quarry where
you have parked.

Continue for a few metres to take the next path going
off right. Climb two little ledges of rock as you go and
stride ahead to a sturdy stile. Go over this and ascend the
stone 'staircase' beyond. At the top go ahead towards
higher ground to reach the elevated metal beacon and
the trig point a few steps beyond.

Walk (north) along the path for a few steps to come
to a signpost where you bear left in the direction of Crag
Foot. Go along the gated way and turn left at a track to

stride downhill. On reaching the road turn to Warton turn right and keep walking until you join the lower route to Warton.

Go along the pavement on the right of the road and then cross and walk on the left to take the signed left turn well before Quicksand Pool Bridge. Pass under the railway bridge, turn right to cross the Pool and step out left along the embanked way known as 'the bund'. Follow this to a stile on the left and continue on the bund as it winds right to come to a signed stile at the foot of Heald Brow.

Turn right and follow the way through woodland to Hollins Lane. Turn right and then right again at the T-junction. Ignoring a road coming in on your right and then another on your left, carry on in the direction of the railway station and, just before you reach it, turn right in the direction of Leighton Moss visitor centre, which you may wish to visit.

*Signpost at the end of 'the bund'*

Then continue a short way along the lane and take a footpath on the right which continues parallel with the road, allowing you to avoid the traffic until you eventually have to rejoin the road. A few steps along turn right to walk the wide causeway across the moss. Continue ahead to pass Grisedale farm on the left and follow the metalled road as it climbs easily to reach Leighton Hall. At the signboard bear left to climb uphill, keeping to the right of a small plantation, and head on up to the seats on the skyline.

Turn right to follow a good path through trees to a minor road. Go right and descend for about 1.6km (nearly 1 mile) to take a bridleway on the right, signed Crag Road. After a very short but steep climb, take the stile on the left into the nature reserve once more and follow the clear path that goes on and on through the trees. Pass through a stile in the wall and continue, watching out for the boulder in the path where the way drops left towards the road. Just before this, turn right along the path taken earlier to return to the car park.

# WALK 3

## Arkholme and Gressingham

| | |
|---|---|
| **Distance** | 11.4km (7 miles) |
| **Time** | 3½ hours |
| **Terrain** | Easy walking all the way, but take care after rain on slippery tree roots across woodland paths |
| **Maps** | OS Explorer OL7 and OL41 |

Park behind the village hall in Arkholme, grid ref 583722. This lies on the south side of the Kirkby Lonsdale road, the B6254, just northeast of the crossroads in the centre of the picturesque village. Rejoin the B6254, which you cross and then walk back to the crossroads. Go on ahead

To see a charming part of Lancashire, visit the quiet village of Arkholme and walk through the delightful surrounding countryside. Here rolling pastures support cattle and innumerable sheep, and deciduous woodlands resound with birdsong. The return is made along the side of the River Lune, which glides below silvery willows and dark alders and whose steep banks drop down to the waterside.

Many of the woods covering these banks are probably ancient, as they grow on land unlikely to have ever been cleared of trees, some of which may be hundreds of years old. The great age of the woods is shown by the wonderful variety of wildflower species they support. The display of bluebells and wild garlic in spring is particularly attractive.

along the B6254 and take the second signposted footpath on the right, which has a tiny stile, just before attractive Bainsbeck House. Walk ahead through a waymarked gate and then a fence, keeping to the right of the outbuildings. Bear slightly left across the pasture to go through a gate at the end of a hedge, and then continue ahead beside a ditch choked with the thrusting leaves of angelica.

At the next waymark cross a footbridge over a stream, left, into a pasture. Strike up the centre of the gently rising ground to climb a stile over a fence and walk on, the fence to your right, towards the cottages at Locka Farm. Go through two gates to join a track and then walk left, passing between several dwellings to join a narrow lane. Turn left to walk the hedged way, Locka Lane, which is lined with flowers in summer, and pass Lower Locka Wood, where in early spring lofty beeches tower over vast carpets of snowdrops. At the T-junction cross to the other side of the B6254 and walk right, using the verge where possible. To your left, through a tracery of leaves, you can see Storrs Hall, a Gothic mansion built in 1848 for Francis Pearson, a Kirkby Lonsdale solicitor. It has a striking, turreted mock-pele tower and an ornate boundary wall.

Just beyond the imposing gates to the hall, pass through a small green gate on your left signposted

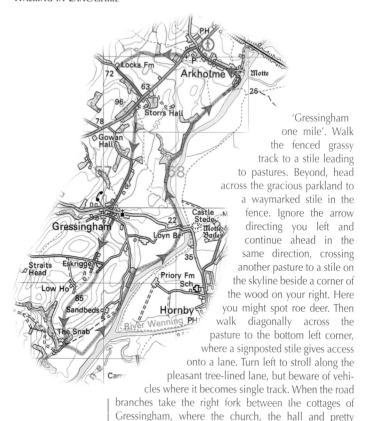

'Gressingham one mile'. Walk the fenced grassy track to a stile leading to pastures. Beyond, head across the gracious parkland to a waymarked stile in the fence. Ignore the arrow directing you left and continue ahead in the same direction, crossing another pasture to a stile on the skyline beside a corner of the wood on your right. Here you might spot roe deer. Then walk diagonally across the pasture to the bottom left corner, where a signposted stile gives access onto a lane. Turn left to stroll along the pleasant tree-lined lane, but beware of vehicles where it becomes single track. When the road branches take the right fork between the cottages of Gressingham, where the church, the hall and pretty houses huddle round falls that are thick with ferns.

The church, St John Evangelist, was rebuilt in 1734, but look for the Norman doorway as well as box pews and a huge Gothic tomb-chest.

Cross the main road and take one step left to walk down a track between a house and a barn into a charming leafy hollow – this is where Gressingham Beck and High Dam Beck meet. Cross these two streams by a long, white-painted footbridge with a pretty fall beneath the second. Stride on to a lane and walk left to pass Far Barn, and then on to a signposted gated track on your right. This might be a good point at which to explore Gressingham before continuing on your walk. ◀

Return to the gated track that leads out of the village and take an awkward stile over a fence beyond stables. Here look left to see Hornby Castle in the distance. Go on beside the fence on your right to cross another (tricky) stile under a huge oak. Climb the sloping pasture ahead to take a similar stile in the top right corner. Then, with the hedge to your right, head down to take a stile to the right of a dwelling and continue along a short track to Lea Lane, where you turn left.

Climb the leafy lane to pass old Eskrigge Hall on the right side of the narrow way. Where the road turns sharp right, pause to enjoy another splendid view of Hornby Castle and its Eagle Tower before swinging right to walk along a tarmacked track. Beside the last house step left to continue along a hidden, sunken grassy track which passes between a hedge and a fence, and which can be wet after rain. Then climb a stile out of the track and into a pasture.

Head on, very slightly left but keeping to the right of two large sycamores, to take a waymarked stile with a signpost beyond. Ignore the track to the right and go ahead, the hedge to your left, over a pasture. Enjoy the

*Bridge at Gressingham*

quiet rolling countryside as you go, following the hedge as it winds a little. Watch out for a waymarked gate on the left that allows you to continue through a farm gate (a very old one at the time of writing) in the right corner and under an oak. Then bear half left, dropping down the slope to take a stile over the middle of a stretch of fencing. Continue, bearing right and keeping to the left of all the buildings until you reach a waymarked gate giving access to a track densely shadowed with trees. Turn left, pass The Snab and walk on a few steps to a signposted sharp-left turn, part of the Lune Valley Ramble, which gives access to a huge pasture beside the River Lune.

Descend the track and bear right, skirting a large pool, to a stile near the bank of the wide river – and now begins the magnificent, well-waymarked upstream riverside walk. ◀ The way comes close to the foot of Sandbeds Lane, which you ignore, and carries on into shady deciduous woodland right beside the river – woodpeckers and jays can be found here. After passing through a small pasture the route then enters more woodland, which you leave by a footbridge. Head on across a large pasture and climb steps onto the road at the left end of

Just before the River Wenning empties its waters into the Lune, and at the right time of the year, you might spot a fly-fisherman casting for salmon.

*Loyn Bridge*

Loyn Bridge. The bridge dates from 1684. Its single carriageway affords the only road crossing of the Lune between Crook of Lune and Kirkby Lonsdale.

Cross the road and go through two stiles to continue on the stiled way beside the river until a stile takes you left over a fence. Here, ignore the path setting off inland, and carry on above and parallel with the river. Follow the waymarks directing you up a steepish slope, and then along the path as it rises through Thrush Gill Wood before joining the riverside pastures again. Press on along the waymarked path, now with small islands between you and the main river.

The stiled way then moves away from the river and continues towards Arkholme. Go past a white house on the left and then through the kissing gate ahead. Beyond, follow the lane as it winds left and climbs to the village. To the right is a road leading to St John's Chapel, standing within the bailey of a Norman motte and bailey which guarded the crossing over the river from the village of Melling. Later a ferry crossed the Lune and at low water you can still see the remains of the ferry steps.

Continue along the road, which is lined with houses bearing 17th- and 18th-century date plaques, pass the village shop and turn right to return to the car park.

# WALK 4

## *Nether Burrow and Leck*

| | |
|---|---|
| **Distance** | 10.5km (6½ miles) |
| **Time** | 3–4 hours |
| **Terrain** | Easy walking all the way; some high stiles to be climbed |
| **Maps** | OS Explorer OL 2 |

Park in the car park of the Highwayman Inn, Nether Burrow, grid ref 614753, 4km (2½ miles) south of Kirkby

The Highwayman Inn at Nether Burrow was once a hunting lodge for the Fenwick family of Burrow Hall – notice the fine coat of arms over the entrance. Standing opposite are the stables, now a private house, and next to them is the old laundry, similarly converted.

This is a most satisfactory walk, taking you through a quiet corner of Lancashire where, for nearly all the route, you are far from the noise and bustle of roads and towns.

The landlord welcomes walkers and likes them to use the space to the south of the inn.

Lonsdale. ◀ From the parking area use one of the wide grass verges to walk north through the tiny village of Nether Burrow, and on for a short distance along the A683 to two-arched Burrow Bridge (constructed 1735) over Leck Beck. Turn right just before the bridge and descend the signposted wooden steps to the bank of the river. Climb the stile ahead and walk upstream as the hurrying water passes through alders, oaks and sycamores. The path moves diagonally right, out into a long pasture, coming beside a mixed plantation and then to Parkside Farm. Take the gate nearest to you, on the far right of the buildings, follow the track as it swings left beyond a barn and continue between outbuildings to take a waymarked gate into pasture.

Continue onwards, with a superb view of Ingleborough ahead, ignoring the gate on

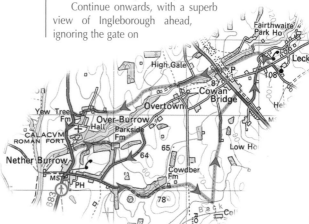

your right into a small pasture and going ahead to a gate onto Woodman Lane. Turn right and stroll along for a little over 1km (nearly ¾ mile) to where the lane turns sharp right. Here, turn left to walk a wide, signposted track in the direction of Cowdber Farm. Continue out into the pastures and then beside Cowdber Wood. Stride on past a dwelling and then the farm to pass through two metal gates. Go ahead for a few steps and through another gate into a pasture, and then through a further gate in the far left corner of the next one. Just beyond, look for an indistinct, slightly raised grassy 'embankment' running northwest. This is the foundation of a Roman road which would have been used by soldiers on their way to the fort sited on a promontory between Leck Beck and the River Lune.

Cross the little stream just beyond the gate and bear right to climb a gate with useful steps tucked into it. Continue on the same diagonal to a stile over a wire fence, and then to another stile over a second wire fence. Keep going to pass through a gate, beyond which you turn left and climb uphill through lovely quiet pastures, and then through a wide gap in the hedge. Go on to find a small gate where the wall and hedge project a little into

*Interested sheep on the Nether Burrow walk*

27

*The Church of St Peter, Leck*

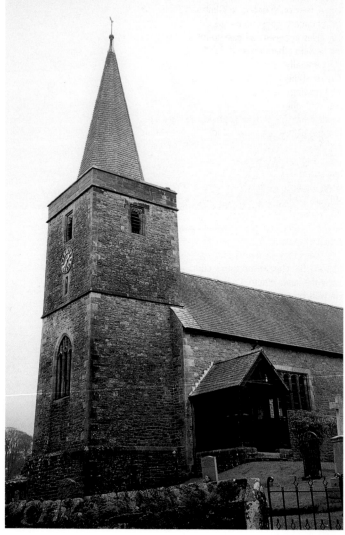

the pasture. Once through the gate keep beside the hedge, now on your left, to climb stone stiles in the next two boundary walls. Then walk diagonally right to a gate that gives access to an easy-to-miss wide, walled track just beyond a barn on your right.

Generally the grassy track is a joy to walk, although it does sometimes become overgrown with brambles. After passing through three gates, climb a stone step stile over the wall on the right and under a large oak. Walk beside the hedge to your left to an awkward gap stile, and continuing in the same direction climb a stile in each of the next two boundary walls (which enclose pastures). Stride ahead to a signposted gap stile to the A65, which you cross. Turn right and take the first left turn to walk along a narrow hedged lane leading towards the village of Leck. Turn right at the crossroads and then follow the road round to the right to come to the Church of St Peter. After a fire the church was rebuilt in 1912 to the original design of Paley and Austin (1878–9).

After a pause here to enjoy the fine parkland all around the church, and the churchyard itself, return along the lane. Where it winds left, take the gap stile in the wall on your right and walk ahead, keeping to the right of a barn. Continue to a stile giving onto a narrow track to the left of a cottage. Walk along this grassy track to the road and cross to a gap stile. Keep going until you come to the side of Leck Beck, where you wind left on the track and, at the gate into a pasture, drop right to walk nearer to the river. (Look for dippers and grey wagtails here.) Move up left from the riverside to walk beside the fenced field on your left and continue to a gap stile. Beyond, go on to pass below the viaduct then follow the path to a further gap stile onto the A65.

Cross the road with care, go through a very narrow gap stile (you may have to walk round it to left or right if it is too narrow) and turn right to walk over the bridge. Turn sharp left immediately to descend a grassy slope to the bank of Leck Beck. Continue along the path, enjoying the dancing Leck to your left, to join a metalled lane. After a short distance along this lane you go over the site of the Roman Road again, but this time there is no trace of it. Ignore a bridge and then a footbridge over the Leck, but before a cattle-grid take a stile on your right. Turn left and walk to the right of a fenced track to the right side of Low Gale. Beyond, move slightly right to climb a small ladderstile and then cross an unusual stone footbridge, with a squeeze stile at its right end, over a tiny tributary of the Leck. Use convenient stones to cross more of the stream – primroses grow here in early spring.

Climb the sloping pasture ahead, keeping beside a fence on your left, then descend to reach a copse on your right. Go on to a difficult-to-spot, awkward stile over the wall at the foot of the slope. Directly ahead stands imposing Burrow Hall, beneath which are believed to be the foundations of the Roman fort of Calacum. Continue ahead, and just before joining a farm track beside a wall, left, observe an unusual stile. Go through the gate by Leck Beck Barn and descend gently to the next gate. Beyond, go up the banking on the right to avoid a ford and continue through a small settlement to the A683. Turn left and walk with care along a short narrow stretch of the road, then use the verges to go over Burrow Bridge and on into the village to rejoin your car.

# WALK 5

## Kirkby Lonsdale and Whittington

| | |
|---|---|
| **Distance** | 10.4km (6½ miles) |
| **Time** | 3–4 hours |
| **Terrain** | Easy walking all the way, except north of Sellet Mill where the path goes along the stream bed |
| **Maps** | OS Explorer OL2 |

Park in the well-signposted car park, grid ref 609786, opposite the supermarket at the southwest end of the

Kirkby Lonsdale stands on high ground overlooking a stunning bend in the River Lune. Its name is believed to be of Danish origin, as the area was settled by these marauding seafarers. Perhaps spend some time exploring the delightful town before setting off on this delectable walk, which takes you for 5km (3 miles) beside the stately river. Enjoy the abundant birdlife before pressing on to the charming village of Whittington. After a short wet walk along a stream bed, where good boots are essential if you are to remain dryshod, the way takes you down over quiet pastures back to the start.

*The Devil's Bridge at Kirkby Lonsdale*

31

## DEVIL'S BRIDGE

One of the legends about how Devil's Bridge got its name claims that an old woman whose cow and pony strayed into the river promised the devil that if he raised a bridge so that her stock could cross, he could have the first thing to do so. Early next morning the old woman threw a bun over the bridge and her mangy dog ran after it. The devil, expecting he would gain a pony or a cow, vanished angrily in flames.

town. Cross the road at the north end of the car park to descend right to pass the Institute on the left. Turn left at the post office along King's Arms Lane. Turn left again into Market Street and wind right through Beck Head. Enter the churchyard to visit St Mary's, built between 1093 and 1130.

Turn right as you leave the building, looking for the eight-sided gazebo in the churchyard which marks the beginning of the terrace overlooking Ruskin's View. Walk along here and see where the River Lune makes its gracious curve, and where you will want to pause. Ruskin described it as, 'One of the loveliest scenes in England – therefore the world'. Next, descend the Radical Steps to reach the side of the river. Walk right and continue along to the spectacular Devil's Bridge where you join a narrow road (to your right is a toilet block).

Cross the road and go through the squeeze stile opposite, just before the bridge. Take the stone steps down to the path beside the river on the south side of the magnificent 15th-century twin-arched bridge known as **Devil's Bridge**.

Continue along the footpath beside the water, walking beneath oak, hawthorn and elm. Pass through the kissing gate just before the next bridge and walk up the slope to the A65. Cross this busy road with care and descend more steps to regain the footpath – the Lune Valley Ramble – and continue downstream. The next bridge carries great pipes over the Lune for the water-board, but just before this bridge bear to the right, go up a small embankment and over a stile. Carry on to pass through a squeeze stile, and after a few metres take another stile on the left where steps lead once more to the riverside.

Continue along the stiled way beside the river, watching out for a waymark that directs you up a slope once more. The way then goes left beside a copse where trees slope steeply down to the river. Descend a short slope to come down to the Lune once more, and look left for a magnificent view of Ingleborough. At the water's edge you might spot a dipper running into the shallows and then back to a shingle reach.

Amble on along the way, sometimes high above the river and sometimes close beside it, to come to a wooden hut for anglers – across the river stands the small village of Nether Burrow. Stroll on along a grassy track with the Lune, now immensely broad, beside you. Press on along the narrow flood bank, which is edged with straggly hawthorns, to take a stile into a track called Coneygarth Lane.

This hedged way is muddy to start with and then, after a gate, becomes grassy as it gradually bears north-west. At its end you cross the B6254 and, after a few steps right, take a stile on the left onto a long grassed track leading to the Church of St Michael the Archangel, with the houses and cottages of Whittington gathered around it.

*The Church of St Michael the Archangel at Whittington*

After a pause here, either in the church or on a seat on a terrace outside, walk on and leave the churchyard by the north gate. Turn left and after a few metres take narrow, sheltered Hosticle Lane on the right, climbing steeply uphill. The lane is walled and supports a hedge 2 metres (6½ feet) high. At the top of the slope look right for another grand view of Ingleborough. Go on past Lane Hall Farm and then descend a little to pass another dwelling. Continue on for a few steps and take a stile on the right just before the lane joins a busy road. Bear slightly right to descend gently, following the waymarks on the fence. Wind round a small wood and continue along its edge to a stile over a fence. Bear left and follow the hedge downhill, with the steep slopes of Sellet Bank to your right.

Go down almost to the corner of the pasture and pass through a gate. Walk ahead to go through a similar gate, and then turn right to reach a signposted stile in the corner of the pasture. Turn sharp left and go through a gate beside a garage and into a narrow, waymarked track. Shortly the path appears to divide and here you take the right branch to cross a stream. Walk on along the right side of the beck – although after heavy rain you may find yourself walking up the stream bed! – eventually crossing the stream to continue a little above the water.

After a short distance the stream disappears and the path becomes dry and good to walk. The hedged way climbs steadily and is particularly pleasant in early spring. Go past several white cottages and turn right at the road. Go past Wood End farmhouse and, just before its huge green slurry tank, turn left to pass through a sign-posted gate. Drop down the pasture to go through a gap stile, and then keep on going down through two metal kissing gates to the side of the A65. Cross with care, then walk right and then left to return to the car park.

# WALK 6

## *Crook of Lune and Aughton*

| | |
|---|---|
| **Distance** | 11.4km (7 miles) |
| **Time** | 3–4 hours |
| **Terrain** | Generally easy walking; steepish road climb from the river to Aughton |
| **Maps** | OS Explorer OL41 |

The Lune is perhaps the finest of Lancashire's rivers. It rises in Cumbria and then idles through its fertile valley in a series of graceful meanders. The calls of waders and ducks are familiar sounds, and the peacefulness of the river is often broken by the loud splash of a leaping salmon. Fine woodlands clothe its banks, and in spring red campion and greater stitchwort contrast pleasingly with wonderful carpets of bluebells.

One of the great bends in this meandering river is called Crook of Lune. In 1835 William Wordsworth praised its loveliness and the beauty spot was a must for all 19th-century travellers, including JMW Turner, for whom it provided the inspiration for a watercolour now hanging in the Courtauld Institute in London.

The parking area is situated above the neck of this great bend in the river, grid ref 522648. From the first car park drop down steps to the riverside and turn left to follow the waymarks for the Lune Valley Ramble. Look back to see the five-arched bridge with its splendid wrought-iron balustrade. This bridge used to carry the railway from Green Ayre in Lancaster to Wennington. Stroll on to a waymarked gate and continue beside the water.

Look across the river to see 18th-century Caton Low Mill, now converted into flats, which produced cotton until the 1970s. Carry on along the stiled and gated way, going by a cascading weir, then pass into delightful woodland where deciduous trees sweep down to the water's edge. The path can be muddy, but it is stepped up and down at awkward places.

Emerge from the trees by a stile and walk on along the edge of the woodland to go under an aqueduct painted white with bright-red rose motifs. Press on through pleasing Applehouse Wood and then leave by steps down to a stile and out of the trees. Go ahead to the edge of the river – here the bank has been extensively repaired after being severely eroded

in the winter floods of 2000. Follow the well-waymarked path as it runs beside a large, horseshoe-shaped meander of the Lune.

*Bluebells and stitch-wort in woodland beside the Lune*

Two-thirds of the way round the great curve the waymarked path moves inland to pass to the right of Over Lune Barn and on to the stile ahead. Beyond, the way continues, half right and slightly raised, across a large pasture to come to the side of the waymarked Lune once more. Walk on to climb the next stile, which is up against the riverbank. Continue ahead along a gated track, following it as it winds round to the left to pass some gritstone cottages. Then climb a steep hedged way, its banks a floral highway in summer, to the pretty village of Aughton – and a seat where you can get your breath back.

Go on uphill in the direction of Halton and take the signposted stile on the left, a short distance along the lane. Head slightly left to the hedge corner and then, on the same diagonal, go up to a stile to the left of a gate. Beyond, climb a long pasture to take a hidden stile in the top fence. A few steps on cross a little footbridge and head up to a stile against the left wall of Far Highfield farm. Walk ahead, with the fence to your right, to a

*Pause for a rest at Aughton*

corner stile, and on to the next, with a hedge to your right. Stroll the stiled way beside the hedge to go through a gate into the farmyard of Middle Highfield.

Go straight ahead to cross an access track and continue on to a gap stile to the right of a ruin. Carry on to the front of another ruin, turn left and then walk ahead to an easy-to-miss stile on the side of the track. At the time of writing this small collection of buildings and ruins was being developed, but the right of way was due to remain and waymarks were to be erected to direct you on your way.

Turn right and remain beside the boundary on your right. Cross a turf bridge over a small stream and go ahead beside a high sturdy wall, on your right, composed of regular blocks of gritstone. Climb a ladderstile and turn right to follow the waymark directing you a couple of steps left through the second of two metal gates.

Follow the fence down on the right and continue where it winds left to a gate in the far-left bottom corner. Beyond, follow a track that soon winds left through the outbuildings of Lower Highfield farm and comes to a signpost.

Descend through two more gates and then go on to another. Cross a turf bridge over a stream and head straight across the pasture to take an iron kissing gate into woodland. Continue on the path through the trees to emerge onto a pasture by a similar kissing gate. Stride ahead over a field to a hedge corner and pause here to enjoy the magnificent view. Continue with the hedge to your right, and remain close beside it to come to a short waymarked 'passage'. This is bordered by a low wall that leaves the hedge on the right just before the dwellings at Hawkshead. Climb the next stile and go on ahead, slightly right, following waymarks that take you down a slope to a stile onto an access track.

Turn right and walk along a way that soon winds left and descends through more woodland. Join narrow Park Lane, turn left and walk on to pass gracious Halton Park. Continue quietly for another 800 metres (½ mile) to a bend at which you reach Low Road. Turn left and walk the pavement for 100 metres, then turn left again to go through a gate on the left and join the track designed for those of limited mobility. This returns you easily to the car park.

## WALK 7

### *Hornby and Melling*

| | |
|---|---|
| **Distance** | 11.4km (7 miles) |
| **Time** | 4 hours |
| **Terrain** | Easy walking all the way, but after rain expect plenty of mud |
| **Maps** | OS Explorer OL2 and OL41 |

Hornby's public car park is on the southwest side of the bridge over the River Wenning, grid ref 585683. Park here and turn left across the bridge so that halfway along you can pause to enjoy the dramatic view of the castle

Hornby's spectacular castle was built between 1849 and 1852, with more work carried out around 1889, but during the 20th century much of the building was demolished and remodelled. Standing behind the castle is the wonderful pele tower, the lower section having been built in the 13th century and the upper part in the 16th. Today, viewed from Hornby Bridge, the picturesque castle looks like a scene from a children's book. St Margaret's Church at Hornby is charming. It has an interesting tower, built in 1514 by Sir Edward Stanley, Lord Monteagle, who died in 1524 leaving the church unfinished. The aisle walls and windows were added in 1817 and altered in 1889.

This walk starts from the village and takes you beside the River Wenning and then the magnificent River Lune. Once under or, depending on the flow of the mighty river, over the fine Loyn Bridge, the way crosses flat pastures where the Lune doubles her journey by winding and bending, horseshoe-like, across the valley floor. The route continues to the delightful village of Melling and then climbs up, away from the noise of the A683, to the fells above. Carrying on over quiet walled pastures, it then descends to the splendid motte and bailey above Loyn Bridge before returning to Hornby.

*Hornby Castle above the River Wenning*

on its hill overlooking the village. At the end of the bridge turn left through a small unsigned gate and walk left. Follow the path as it winds right to continue along a

reinforced path with the river to your left. Climb the steps over the low floodbank to your right to pass through a gap stile on your left into a pasture. Beyond the next stile continue along the riverbank, now lined with alders.

About 1.4km (just under 1 mile) from the bridge at Hornby the Wenning flows into the River Lune, and here you turn right to walk upstream of the Lune. After another 1.6km (a mile or so) the path passes below a slope covered with brambles and hawthorn bushes, then climbs the slope into a pasture and carries on above the river to arrive at a waymark. Here a notice explains that if the river is in spate then the continuing path below Loyn Bridge will be impassable. If this is the case there is a white waymark directing you right, away from the right of way, to join the road. Here you turn left and descend to the start of the bridge to go through a stile beside the gate on the right.

If the river is not in spate, then go on along the clear path to a stile into woodland. Here in spring the steeply sloping bank to your right is carpeted with yellow saxifrage, wood anemones and bluebells. Carry on beside the river to a ladderstile that allows you to go under Loyn Bridge, which has carried traffic to Gressingham and Arkholme since the 17th century. On the far side of the bridge, on the right, steps leads up to the footpath.

Before you set off along the indistinct path, notice the mound to your right. This is the site of a motte and bailey used by the Normans as a defensive position guarding the river crossing. But save your visit to the site until your return, when the right of way takes you close beside it.

For 1.2km (¾ mile) walk on parallel with the river and close beside an embankment on your right. Soon after the embankment begins to curve slightly right, walk on half left to cross an easy-to-miss concrete tractor bridge over a stream, the Old Lune, that emerges from the ground and flows east, away from the Lune. Look ahead and to the right to see the village of Melling and, behind it, Ingleborough with its top often in cloud. From the tractor bridge walk ahead in the same general direction across a large pasture to a metal gate in the fence.

Continue on to negotiate several tiny ditch-like streams. You may have to move to the left to cross them, and then right again to go on along the general line of the walk. Look ahead to see two railway viaducts and a bridge – aim for the larger, many-arched viaduct to the right, nearer to Melling.

Stride ahead over the pasture, keeping to the right of the Old Lune, to reach the corner of a hedge where there is a prominent waymark. Go on, following the well-waymarked route until the path comes to two stiles close to the water's edge. Once over the stiles follow the track, keeping to the side of the fence on your right. Go through the waymarked kissing gate and along the farm track that runs below the railway embankment on the Melling side of the viaduct.

Follow the track as it winds steadily right, and when it comes to the A683 turn right and walk 100 metres into the village of Melling. You might like to visit the church and view the lovely old houses that line the main road here. If not, continue the route by taking the first left between Melling Hall and the vicarage, well before the church, to walk up Wennington Road.

Continue uphill on the pavement on the left to come to a footpath sign. A few metres beyond there is another footpath sign, high on a lamp post. This directs you across the road to a path that slopes up through trees to a gate to a large steep pasture. Go through the gate and keep beside the hedge on your left until you reach a stile through a fence on the left. Beyond the stile continue in the same general direction, uphill, to a further stile in the fence ahead.

Continue on uphill, bearing slightly left, to a waymarked stile to the left of a small copse. Walk ahead to cross a turf bridge to a narrow tarmacked road. Here you turn right and climb gently to Lodge Farm – to the left stretch the hills of the Forest of Bowland. Bear left to walk along the side of the farmhouse, pass through a gate and walk ahead, dropping downhill to climb a stile. Follow the way as it winds left, keeping to the right side of a sunken track, then go on beside a very steep-sided, tree-lined gill.

Where the gill swings left and you reach the outbuildings and huge silage pit before Park House farm, take the gated cart track on the right. Climb gently up through the breezy pasture to where the track divides. Here turn left and go on the pleasing way to pass through a narrow strip of woodland. Emerge onto a pasture and walk for a short distance beside the wall on your right, then take a waymarked stile on your right. Continue up the other side of the wall to climb an obvious ladderstile. Beyond, turn right and follow the wall round on your right to reach a waymarked gate. Go through the gate and walk ahead for a few steps to join a track where you turn left and drop downhill to the left side of a conifer plantation. Continue downhill, keeping beside the wall on the right almost to the road, and then walk a few metres left to a gate to the A683, which you cross with care.

*Motte and bailey beside Loyn Bridge*

This ancient fortification occupied an ideal defensive position overlooking the Lune. Today it supports magnificent beech trees and Scots pine, and in spring its slopes are covered with bluebells.

Walk right for 150 metres, using the verge where possible, to a signposted stiled footpath on your left. Follow the path left towards Holme Head farm, keeping outside the farm fence and with a huge slurry tank to your left. Go on to a small gate on the left at the corner of the pasture, with the footpath sign on the far side. Carry on to pass through a metal gate, then climb a slope and take the second gate on the left.

Go ahead to come to the dry moat of the motte and bailey mentioned earlier. ◄ Walk round above the moat, which stops at a point where once the River Lune flowed along its side.

Walk on to drop down the slope, past a modern defensive building – a 1939–45 wartime pillbox – to a stile to the lane to Loyn Bridge. Turn left and walk for 500 metres to join the A-road, where another 600 metres brings you back to the parking area.

# WALK 8

## *Low Bentham*

| | |
|---|---|
| **Distance** | 11.4km (7 miles) |
| **Time** | 4 hours |
| **Terrain** | Easy walking |
| **Maps** | OS Explorer OL41 |

This walk takes you through rolling pastures with extensive views over Lancashire and Yorkshire. Although your walking starts in Yorkshire, for most of the way you are in a lovely quiet corner of Lancashire. Old field paths linking one farm with another were in use long before today's connecting roads were constructed. The route passes through several deciduous woods where, in spring, trees slant down slopes to small streams and the floor is covered with a vast carpet of bluebells. If you complete the walk a week or so later you will hear the haunting cry of the curlew and the wild musical whistle of the green plover that nests in the pastures. Go warily along hedgerows or over long grass where pheasants may nest, the females lying so still that you can pass without them blinking an eye.

This walk entails climbing many stiles and passing through farm gates – not all of which are waymarked.

Park in the free car park at Low Bentham, grid ref 651694, which lies on the south side of Low Bentham Road. Turn left out of the car park and walk west through the village, crossing the bridge over the River Wenning flowing north. Continue under the railway bridge and walk on with care to turn left into Eskew Lane, immediately beyond the Punch Bowl Inn (dated 1670). Unexpectedly the River Wenning is now on the right – but flowing south under a splendid arched bridge. A look at your map solves the puzzle – this is where the river makes a large S-shaped curve.

Walk along the lane for 200 metres to take the sign-posted stiled footpath on the left. Continue ahead to pass through a gateless gap, and then veer slightly left (east) away from the wall and hedge on your right. Climb the long sloping pasture and pass a house, Cloudsbank, on your left, then carry on for a few steps to a signposted stile to the right of a gate onto Mill Lane.

Turn right to continue along the lane and take the second signposted way on the right – from this good track you have a grand view of High and Low Bentham. Continue to the yard of Kirkbeck, a gracious farmhouse dated 1676 – a monastery stood here earlier and its stone was used to construct the farm. Just before the house follow the waymark directing you right. Go slightly left across a small yard and take a stepped stile over a wall to the left of a barn. Descend a small pasture, slightly left again, and cross a wooden footbridge over Eskew Beck and into Lancashire. Climb up the slope through woodland, where the path is deeply littered with leaves, and go on to a stile. Keeping beside the beck, deep in its wooded gill, continue left and cross the next stile. Keep ahead over a pasture to a stepped stile to Mewith Lane (here in early autumn

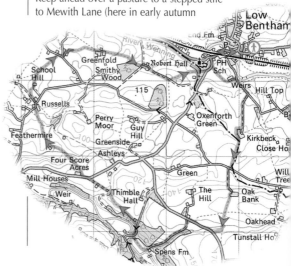

harebells flower in profusion), turn right, and then take the next left turn, which is a track to Oak Bank farm.

Walk in front of the farmhouse and turn left to a gate just beyond. Pass below two magnificent horsechestnut trees shadowing a yard to go through a waymarked wicket gate onto a pasture. Cross to the far right corner where there is a white post (out of sight at first). Climb a stile and cross a plank footbridge and go on ahead in the same direction to take the next stile. Turn right beyond it, walk to a gate onto Spen Brow and turn right. Stroll along the lane until you reach Spen Lodge on the right, with its white studded door.

Take the gate opposite the lodge and head over the pasture to the side of Spen Gill Wood. Walk downhill with the plantation to your left, taking care here as the ground can be very wet all the way down beside the trees. Go through the muddy gateway to Spens Farm and turn immediately right through a small gate. Carry on over a lawn to a stile, and then strike left to join the track through this open area. There is walled woodland to the right, and enormous high slopes supporting more deciduous woodland to the left. Go on to join Furnessford Road.

*Wooden footbridge over Eskew Beck*

Ingleborough seen from walk

Turn right and climb the hill to a signposted footpath leading left into a wood. Descend a slope to step across a tiny stream and go on, keeping to the left of the fence that forms the boundary between the wood and the farm. Follow the narrow path, which keeps well above the River Hindburn, as it leads to a waymarked stile. (Here, if you can see a bull in the field, ignore the stile and keep going along the path to the far end of the wood.) Beyond the stile continue in the same general direction (northwest) to cross to a stile in a hedge. (If, because of the bull, you have arrived at the end of the wood, go through a gate, head up beside the hedge and then descend the slope.) Go ahead and then drop down the slope to a ladderstile to the right of a reinforced track. Continue ahead along the track, passing to the right of Mashiters, and walk the lengthy access track to Long Lane, which you cross.

Walk a few metres left to go through a signposted gate and continue ahead to a stile in the left corner of the pasture. Stride on ahead over a rough pasture to a rather awkward stile in the far corner. Beyond, descend an old sunken way to a clapper bridge over Clear Beck. Walk to the end of the fence on your left and climb the stile in the corner. Press on to climb a small stile over a fence to the right of a barn, then go on to take a stile in the hedge on the right. Once over, walk the sunken track ahead and follow it as it swings slightly left and uphill to a stile on the right beneath an oak. Head on across the pasture to another stile and then take a little stile immediately on your left. Halfway along this large pasture follow a sunken track that leads slightly right to a gate to a lane.

Turn right and pass a farmhouse called Russells (dated 1682). Turn left, just beyond, into another lane in the direction of Meggs farm, with extensive views over Lancashire. Once past the access track to the farmhouse on your left, climb a stile over the wire on your right and walk on to a stile in the left corner of the hedge. Then go ahead over another stile over a fence, and on ahead to a stone stepped stile to the access track to a dwelling. Turn left and pass through a wicket gate at the left end of the barn of School Hill farmhouse. Continue ahead for a few steps and climb a stile in a hawthorn hedge. Head diagonally down, right, to a large tree in the middle of the pasture and then go straight down to a stile in the hedge. Beyond, walk ahead to cross two more stiles to reach a narrow lane.

Walk right and after 20 metres take the signposted footpath on the left, the second of two tracks, to Higher Perries farm. Turn right beyond a barn to reach a waymarked stile under an oak and go diagonally across the pasture to the far left corner. Walk ahead to a waymarked stile in the hedge opposite, and continue slightly right to wind round a pasture to a gate to Greenfold farm. Go ahead in front of the house, cross the access track and take the arrowed gate in front of you into a pasture.

Continue slightly left across the pasture to reach a stile and then a footbridge over a beck. Climb the wooden steps to continue on an indistinct way to a stile.

## ROBERT HALL

From here you can see ancient Robert Hall, with its mullioned windows and square chimney. It was once a fortified dwelling belonging to the Harringtons and the Cantsfields, and has a magnificent beamed barn with a huge fireplace and an arch in its north wall, probably the relic of an earlier building on the site. It also has a priest hole, and for many years had its own chapel and priest. It is rumoured that Katherine Parr, later to become Henry VIII's queen, visited here. The house is still occupied.

Climb the open pasture to continue in front of **Robert Hall** and then press on along the farm track for 450 metres. Here leave the track to pass through a gateless gap on the left, and walk on in the same general direction for another 450 metres, gradually drifting left to a stile into pleasant woodland. Drop down the steep but stepped slope, cross the footbridge over the River Eskew just before it joins the River Wenning, and walk the footpath beyond to join Eskew Lane. Turn left, continue to the

Punch Bowl Inn, turn right, go under the railway bridge and continue to cross the bridge over the Wenning. Walk on through Low Bentham and turn right along Low Bentham Road to the car park on your right.

# WALK 9

## *Sunderland Point*

| | |
|---|---|
| **Distance** | 8km (5 miles) |
| **Time** | 2–3 hours |
| **Terrain** | Level walking; the way through the vegetation along the shore and across the pastures can be wet after heavy rain; it is very stony around the point |
| **Maps** | OS Explorer 296 |

Walk the shore above tidal flats to wind round Sunderland Point, then continue through the tiny hamlet of Sunderland and on over pastures to return to the parking area. Sunderland looks much as it must have done in the 18th century, when it was developed by a local man, Robert Lawson, as a port for Lancaster's thriving trade with the West Indies. Legend says that the first bales of cotton ever to be landed in Britain arrived here.

The lane from Overton to the cluster of picturesque dwellings crosses mudflats and saltings, and when it floods at high tide the hamlet can only be reached by footpaths. In spring the carolling of skylarks and the evocative call of courting curlews comes from the pastures. If the tide is flowing you can see oystercatchers, redshanks, dunlin and ringed plover feeding incessantly on the rapidly disappearing mudflats. Large numbers of shelduck move restlessly from shore to pasture.

This walk starts at Middleton Sands. These are approached by Carr Lane, a long, narrow, winding way that leads from Middleton and ends at a small parking area at the beach, grid ref 414572. Walk south along the signposted bridleway, a roughish path that can be wet after rain or a very high tide. Generally when the tide is in water laps over the fine turf and fills the tidal trenches to your right. Enjoy the far-reaching view over the waters of the bay to Knott End and Fleetwood and the glorious expanse of sky with its ever-changing pattern of cloud. Gorse, frequently covered with yellow blossoms, grows up against the sea-defence wall.

Continue on along the path which leads you to a gate to a farm track. Carry on along the shore, passing a farm on your left, to come to a signposted and gated bridleway, The Lane, which turns inland and leads to the centre of the hamlet of Sunderland. The walk presses on along the shore path to a signposted step stile into a low-walled enclosure.

Here is buried a slave called Sambo, once a sea captain's cabin boy. He came to Sunderland in 1736, and having died of what is thought to have been a fever, was not allowed to be buried in consecrated ground. On his grave, at the time of writing almost covered by painted and inscribed stone slabs, is a plaque bearing the following poem written by a Rev. James Watson in 1796:

Full sixty years the angry winter's wave,
Has thundering dashed this bleak and barren shore,
Since Sambo's head laid in this lonely grave,
Lies still and ne'er will hear their turmoil more.

Full many a sandbird chirps upon the sod,
And many a moonlight elfin round him trips,
Full many a summer's sunbeam warms the clod
And many a teeming cloud upon him drips.

But still he sleeps – till the awakening sounds,
Of the Archangels trump new life impart,
Then the Great Judge his approbation founds,
Not on man's colour but his worth of heart.

'Sandbirds' still chirp and fresh flowers regularly adorn this quiet corner.

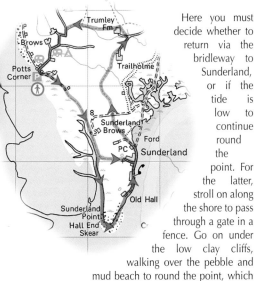

Here you must decide whether to return via the bridleway to Sunderland, or if the tide is low to continue round the point. For the latter, stroll on along the shore to pass through a gate in a fence. Go on under the low clay cliffs, walking over the pebble and mud beach to round the point, which is guarded by Plover Scar lighthouse. Hawthorn bushes line the sheltered east bank. From this side of the point a wide expanse of the Lune estuary stretches ahead, and

*Looking across the Lune estuary to Glasson*

53

*Sunderland Hall*

you can just glimpse the masts of the many boats at Glasson Dock, which eventually took away all Sunderland's trade.

Carry on to pick up a pebbly path and then join a narrow grassy promenade to go past picturesque Sunderland Hall (dated 1683), which has the air of a colonial house in the West Indies. Walk on past a terrace of cottages, one of which is called Cotton Tree Cottage (dated 1751) after the black poplar that once shadowed it and which each summer was laden with cottony blossom. Alas, it was blown down in a storm in the 1990s, having survived previous storms for more than 200 years. Interesting information about the poplar can be found on a notice fixed to a portion of the old trunk outside the cottages. Then you come to the end of the bridleway, The Lane, and Upsteps Cottage where Sambo died.

Continue along the shore, passing another terrace of houses and a narrow alley with a tiny cottage built in 1645. At the end of the terrace you can see the posts marking the route of the tide road from Overton to the hamlet. Ignore these and continue walking ahead along a track lying up against the flood-defence bank on your left to reach a white-painted ladderstile and climb up it onto the banking. Descend steps down the other side into a pasture and head diagonally right to take the sometimes wet way over to a footbridge in the far corner. Turn right and walk beside a drainage ditch on your right to cross the next footbridge. Carry on in the same direction to cross another. Here in spring you might see a reed bunting stammering and stuttering its nuptial song on top of a hawthorn bush.

Stride on, moving away from the dyke to an obvious ladderstile in the fence ahead (from here you have a good view of Black Combe). Walk clockwise round the edge of the field as directed by the arrow. Ignore a gate and go on round to climb a tiny ladder of steps and then up onto the flood embankment. Walk right to go through a gate, continue along a wide track and pass left of Trailholme farm. Carry on where the track becomes metalled and watch out for the signposted gap stile, right, which you take through the hedge onto the access track to Trailholme farm. Turn left and in 200m take the sign-posted stile on the left to Low Road. Where the track branches keep to the right fork to pass all the buildings of Marsh Lea farm.

Shortly, at the junction of tracks, climb the sign-posted stile on the left. Walk ahead to a wooden stile over the fence and slant right to a stile beside a gate in the far right corner of the pasture. Beyond, ignore a gate on the left, and go ahead to a hidden ladderstile in the left corner of the pasture where two hedges meet. Once over, walk beside an outbuilding on your left and then wind left to join the access track to the building. Turn right and walk a short distance to join Carr Lane, where you turn left to rejoin your car.

# WALK 10

## *Glasson and the Lancaster Canal*

| | |
|---|---|
| **Distance** | 10.4km (6½ miles) |
| **Time** | 3–4 hours |
| **Terrain** | Easy walking all the way |
| **Maps** | OS Explorer 296 |

This walk takes you along the Lancashire Coastal Way from Conder Green to Glasson Basin and Dock. It continues beside the quiet waters of the Glasson branch of the Lancaster Canal, and at the second lock stone bridge of this short waterway makes a diversion to allow you to see Double Bridge over the mainline canal. After a pleasant walk along the towpath of this older waterway the route returns you over quiet pastures to Conder Green.

The car park, grid ref 457562, is on the site of the old Conder Green railway station (there are toilets here). To reach this parking area, turn off the Lancaster-to-Cockerham road (A588) by the Stork Hotel and continue west to the end of the minor road.

Leave the car park and walk southwest along the Lancashire Coastal Way, opened in September 1991. The path follows the route of the Lancaster–Glasson Dock railway, a branch line of the former London and North Western Railway, which opened in 1883 (its rails were removed in 1962).

Cross the bridge over the River Conder and stroll the hedged way. Through gaps in the trees you can enjoy extensive views over the estuary of the River Lune to Bazil Point and Sunderland. Continue beside the splendid sea wall into the village of Glasson and then join the road. Opposite the Victoria Inn walk onto the

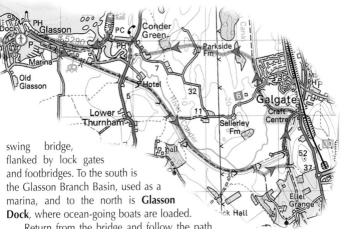

swing bridge, flanked by lock gates and footbridges. To the south is the Glasson Branch Basin, used as a marina, and to the north is **Glasson Dock**, where ocean-going boats are loaded.

Return from the bridge and follow the path, now on the right just beyond a café, which takes you beside the canal basin. Follow the signpost directions to walk the towpath. To your left a small gate gives access to Christ Church, which has a fine bell tower and was built 14 years after the canal. Immediately after the church you pass under Brows Bridge, a skew bridge, no 8.

Stroll on along the waterway, lined in summer with meadowsweet, kidney vetch, comfrey and marsh woundwort, and pass below the railed Brick Kiln Bridge, no 7. Stride on to walk below Thurnham Bridge, no 6, beyond which stands Thurnham Mill, once a water-powered cornmill with a channel of water from the River Conder to drive its machinery. Today it is a hotel and restaurant with an attractive canalside tavern.

## GLASSON DOCK

Glasson Dock was developed when the River Lune silted up in the 1780s and ships were unable to reach St George's Quay at Lancaster. They took coal to Cornwall, bringing back china clay; timber, wood pulp and iron ore also arrived at the dock. The Glasson branch of the canal was opened in 1826.

*Glasson church*

By the old mill is the first in a flight of six locks before the mainline canal. Each lock has a small weir at the side to take off excess water and a footbridge giving access to the opposite bank. Continue beside the cut and its locks, passing below bridge nos 5, 4 and 3. Once you have passed below bridge no 2 (number on its far side) turn immediately left off the towpath to take a gap stile, and wind round left to cross the canal bridge.

*This bridge is twice the width of other canal bridges and has a wall along the middle that serves as a boundary between two farms.*

Walk ahead along a wide cart track and follow it where it winds left. At the next corner, where there is an ancient gatepost, climb the easy-to-miss stile on the left off the track and into a pasture. Walk down beside the hedge on your right, and beyond the next stile continue down a grooved way which brings you to Double Bridge over the mainline canal. ◀

*Turnover Bridge at the junction of the Glasson branch and Lancaster Canal*

There is no access to this tantalising part of the towpath, so you need to turn left and walk beside the hedge on your right to a squeeze stile that brings you to cobbled Junction Bridge, no 1, a turnover bridge. (This type of bridge allowed a boat to continue without the horse being disconnected.)

Cross the fine bridge and follow the towpath beside the mainline waterway, passing the lock-keeper's cottage on your left. Just before bridge no 86 is Galgate Marina. Head on beneath the bridge to come to the Conder Aqueduct, bridge no 87. Here you can lean over to see the River Conder hurrying beneath the low arch, and note the buttresses and curving walls. You then pass below Ellel Hall Bridge, no 88, and press on until you are opposite the last dwelling on the outskirts of the village of Galgate. Take the signposted stile in the hedge on your left.

Beyond, strike ahead across the meadow and then bear right beside the fence, beyond a very wet area, to climb a stile and continue beside Forerigg Wood, now on your left. Enter the wood by a stile and walk the narrow path through the trees to leave by another. Head up the pasture to go over a metal stile tucked into a bend in the hedge almost opposite. Beyond this follow a short path through rough vegetation, a hedge to your right, to a stile beside a gate on your right. Continue ahead, with the hedge to your right, to go through a waymarked gap stile in the hedge and beside a gate. Turn left to walk to Parkside Farm, passing through the farm buildings and the yard to a gap stile to the right of a gate.

Continue ahead with a fenced hedge to your right, take a narrow stile, cross a footbridge and then climb another stile, all in a few metres. Beyond, turn left and walk on with the fenced hedge to your left to pass the back of Webster's Farm. Go on to climb a stile tucked up beside a building on your left and onto narrow Galgate Road.

Turn right and walk the lane to join the A588. Turn left and then right in front of the Stork Inn to walk the quiet minor road to rejoin your car.

# WALK 11

## *Cockerham and Cockersand Abbey*

| | |
|---|---|
| **Distance** | 12km (7½ miles) |
| **Time** | 4 hours |
| **Terrain** | Easy walking; some muddy farm tracks |
| **Maps** | OS Explorer 296 |

Walk the quiet marshland pastures named after the farmers who reclaimed them from the sea, and then stroll on along the side of the Cocker Channel to watch the innumerable waders that feed in the exposed salt marsh and estuarine mud. The route brings you to the remains of Cockersand Abbey, often wreathed in a sea mist that adds to its magical, mysterious atmosphere.

Start from the car park by Cockerham parish hall, grid ref 466521. This lies towards the south end of the village on the B5272. There are toilets at the junction of the B5272 and the A588, opposite the Manor public house.

From the north side of the parish hall take the paved track leading to St Michael's Church. The church has a solid, ashlar-built Perpendicular tower, the remainder being built in 1910 by the noted architects Austin and Paley. Continue on through the churchyard, where there is believed to be an unmarked plague pit in which those who died of the Black Death were buried (1349).

Leave by the kissing gate beyond the church, turn right and walk along the reinforced way to the A588. Turn left and keep to the pavement for 250 metres, then cross with care and take the signposted stile into a large pasture. Carry on beside a ditch on the right and cross stiles and footbridges, all waymarked, to come parallel with buildings belonging to a parachute club. Cross a concrete track and head slightly left into a clump of trees

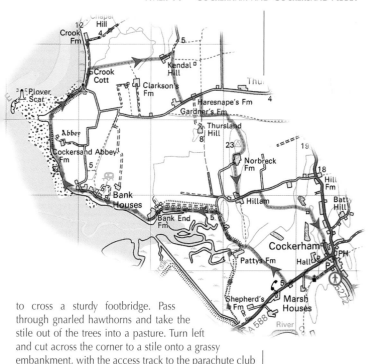

to cross a sturdy footbridge. Pass
through gnarled hawthorns and take the
stile out of the trees into a pasture. Turn left
and cut across the corner to a stile onto a grassy
embankment, with the access track to the parachute club
and Pattys Farm below. Beyond, Cockerham Marsh
stretches away into the distance.

Turn right to walk the embankment as far as you can
and then drop down to the access-track part of the
Lancashire Coastal Way. Cross at the road, climb another
embankment and walk left towards the estuary. At the
end of the high-level way, descend left to the signpost by
Bank End Farm to follow the coastal path along the left
side of the farmhouse.

Follow the track as it winds right and leave it where
it bears right into the caravan site. Here, keep left of a
fence – the marshy environs of the Cocker Channel are
to your left. Step out along the lovely raised embankment, with many sightings of waders probing the muddy

edges of the river. Press on along the way, from where you can see bright-red plates of sandstone on the shore.

About 900 metres (just over ½ mile) from Bank End you approach the crenellated chapter house which (plus two piles of stone and the atmosphere!) is all that remains of Cockersand Abbey. ◄

*Once, when this tiny part of Lancashire was a small clay island, just above the winter floods and surrounded by undrained marshland, it was a home for lepers and was approached over the sands.*

Return to the coastal path and pause to look out at the Plover Light, standing on the far edge of Plover Scar and marking the deep-water channel of the River Lune. Carry on along the sea wall and continue where it becomes tarmacked and reaches Slack Lane.

Cross and walk on along the side of the estuary for 250 metres to pass Crook Cottage on your right. Immediately beyond, take the signposted stile on the right and walk ahead down a hedged ginnel to another similar stile. Go ahead over a pasture to pass through a gap in the hedge and then onto a footbridge over the dyke. Cross the next dyke on a plank and keep parallel with the hedge to your left. Look right to see Tomlinson's Farm and Clarkson's Farm, both named after early reclaimers of the marsh.

*The Chapter House at Cockersand Abbey*

Go over the next two stiles, now with the fence to your right. Press on over a footbridge and head on to climb the next stile. Pass on through a way that can be muddy, and once over a dyke try to avoid the worst of the cattle poaching to take a stile beside a gate to the left of Kendal Hill farm (this was an island before the reclamation of the marsh). Cut the corner tightly to a stile on the right giving onto a metalled lane.

Walk left to where the lane swings left and take the waymarked gate on the right. Wind close to the left side of the garden of a bungalow to pass through a gate, and turn left to take another gate onto a wide farm track. Where the track swings left, go ahead through a gate, over a field and carry on to climb more stiles to pass left of Gardner's Farm and join Moss Lane.

Go left and walk on for 250 metres to take a track on the right in the direction of Thursland Hill (also once an island). Just before the gate – it has lots of notices on it saying that beyond is private land – turn left to walk with a ditch and hedge to your right.

Carry on over several stiles and two footbridges. Just beyond the second bridge and the next stile, look for an easy-to-miss plank bridge and a stile through the hedge on your right into a pasture. Walk ahead, and at the far

*Embanked way along the side of the Lune estuary*

63

left corner go through a gate and join a farm track that winds right, uphill, with fine views across to the Bowland Fells. This good track continues beside a pond on your right, much favoured by mallards. The track winds round to the right and then left to Norbreck Farm.

Keep ahead through the farm buildings and then bear right in front of a white house. Immediately opposite this attractive dwelling go left and take the right of two gates. Continue ahead over several stiled pastures to Hillam Farm. Pass through the cobbled yard between the farmhouse and its outbuildings to join Hillam Lane and turn left. Walk on for 400 metres to a signposted gate on the right. Beyond, walk the farm track, following it when it begins to wind left. Go through a gate and then walk ahead to a footbridge over Hasty Beck. Press on ahead to a tall stone, painted bright yellow and below a horse-chestnut tree, and then climb a sturdy stile beyond it into the garden of a cottage. Strike across the corner to take a gate on the left, wind right to the next stile and then join a track. Stroll on, and where the track turns left seek out the hidden stile on your right. With the fence to the right, walk ahead to the next stile and then climb uphill beside the hedge on your left to a stile into woodland. Go on to pass through a builder's yard and along a wide track to the A588. Cross, and turn left and then right to return to the car park.

## WALK 12

### *Abbeystead and Dolphinholme*

| | |
|---|---|
| **Distance** | 13km (8 miles) |
| **Time** | 4 hours |
| **Terrain** | Easy walking all the way |
| **Maps** | OS Explorer OL41 |

This attractive route takes you alongside the River Wyre to charming Lower Dolphinholme, returning over higher pastures. Both the outward and the return route pass through splendid deciduous woodland. If you walk this way in early May the floor of each copse, plantation or wood is a blaze of blue – a wall-to-wall carpet of bluebells. Many narrow lanes are crossed, and when these peter out good footpaths continue on, often leading to woods where tiny streams, hidden by dense vegetation, race through steep-sided gills. Many of the streams hurry to join the River Wyre. Throughout this walk the noise of the motorway and other major roads seems far away.

Just east of Abbeystead Reservoir and the hamlet of Abbeystead, cross Stoops Bridge and turn right into a minor road. Park in a grassy area, grid ref 564544, beside the Marshaw Wyre river. Turn left out of the parking area and cross Stoops Bridge. The Marshaw Wyre flows below, and once it is united with the Tarnbrook Wyre they flow into Abbeystead Reservoir. Walk on through the pleasing village of Abbeystead, which gives its name to the reservoir and is itself named after an earlier abbey established by the monks of Furness Abbey.

*Stoops Bridge, Abbeystead*

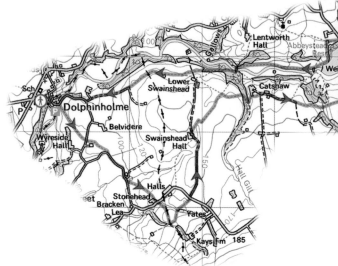

Beyond the village climb the hill under lofty beeches and ascend the ladderstile on the left at the end of the crash barrier. Head on over the pasture, away from the wood on your left, to go through a gate to Far House Barn farm. Bear left as directed on the farm's concrete track and descend a pasture. Where the track winds right, walk to a gate on the left signed 'Footpath'. Descend a few steps beside the reservoir and stand at the corner of the towering dam to see the lovely sheet of the water, softened and shadowed by fine deciduous woodland.

Walk beside the stepped fish-pass and enjoy the architecture of the reservoir. Looking through the trees ahead you can see the fine weir over which cascades foaming water, carrying on down the valley as the River Wyre. Go on through a small copse, ignore the bridge across the river, and walk along the path to pass through a waymarked gate onto the concrete track once more.

Continue on with the River Wyre to your left to pass a small building where there is a moving memorial

plaque. This commemorates the tragedy of 23 May 1984, when villagers from the Parish of St Michael's on Wyre died of asphyxiation during a visit to the water-treatment building at the reservoir.

Where the concrete track ends another good track and then a path carry on, well waymarked, beside the river. Go through a gate, soon to climb slightly to the right, and carry on beside a fence on the left until you reach Long Bridge. Cross the bridge and bear right along a waymarked path with the Wyre now to your right. At a Y-junction of narrow grassy paths, take the left branch to pass through an area of young planting, and then climb through delightful mature oak woodland to a stile into a large pasture. Beyond, turn right to walk to a stile over a fence, keeping well below Lower Swainshead farm. Walk on to cross a ditch by a footbridge and continue ahead towards a barn. Once past the barn take the stile ahead to go through a gate onto a good reinforced track. Follow this ahead and also where it swings right to a gate in the far right corner of the second pasture. Walk on to join Wagon Road, and then turn left and descend below very tall oaks to Lower Dolphinholme, sited on both banks of the River Wyre.

Return to the foot of Wagon Road to take a stepped way to a footpath on the right through woodland. Climb a stile into open pasture and walk ahead to the stile on the other side, just before a row of Scots pine and some deciduous trees. Beyond, walk the path below the trees

Spending some time in the tree-surrounded hollow of Lower Dolphinholme is recommended. There is virtually nothing to remind you now of a worsted mill that once sent smoke up its very tall chimney into the surrounding higher land, although all the various buildings for the workers in this once-industrial corner have been restored.

*A grassy trod below an avenue of may*

and then wind left to a stile in a fence. Carry on over a narrow pasture to cross a footbridge giving access again to a higher part of Wagon Road.

Cross the road, take the stile opposite and walk ahead beside the wall of a dwelling. Then descend a pasture to take a stile up against woodland in the far right corner. Cross a footbridge and turn right to climb a stile onto Tinker's Lane. Turn left and go along the quiet narrow hedged way. Just past a house take a signposted footpath on the left leading to a footbridge over narrow Street Brook. Beyond an immediate stile continue through a small planting of trees to a waymarked stile. Follow the telegraph poles across a pasture to a gate, then walk a good track that eventually turns right to pass through a large gate. Bear left and go on through the yard of Stonehead farm to Long Lane.

Turn left and in a few steps climb the stile opposite the farmhouse. Descend a steepish rough slope and then wind right. Pass under a wire to take a footbridge over a stream. Head away from the stream to cross to the far left corner of a large pasture. Go through a gateless gap and turn left up a rather wet sunken track. Beyond a gate pass a ruin on your left and bear round to the left to walk a wide grassy way between two rows of hawthorns. Descend to ford the little stream crossed earlier and walk ahead along the bank of the continuing wet sunken track. Go through either of two gates to walk ahead to Long Lane once more.

Cross Long Lane and walk along Waste Lane, a narrow, low-hedged reinforced track from where there is a fine view of the hills. Follow the lane past the farm buildings of Swainshead Hall, cross the cattle-grid at the end of the outbuildings and take the waymarked gate off the track on the right. Walk diagonally downhill over a rough pasture to a stile in the right corner. Walk on parallel with the fence to your left to come level with a stile on your left. Ignore this, but turn right here and walk along a little bank, the foundation of an old hedge, until you reach a gap in the bank. Then bear left and veer slightly right towards a stile into Mark Holme Wood.

Turn right and descend gently through oak woodland, with a very steep drop on your left down into Hall Gill. Carry on the path to cross a footbridge over the little stream. Beyond, follow the path left and uphill to climb a stile. Turn right and climb further uphill to pass in front of Catshaw Hall, taking a stile, just to the left of an electricity pole, onto a track with a large barn beyond.

Walk right, ignoring the track that goes off right, and carry on to pass Little Catshaw. Where the track then swings right, go ahead, keeping the waymarked fence to your right, and descend a pasture to a stile in the corner. Go down steps to cross a footbridge in a tiny gill, and bear very slightly right across the next pasture to take another stile into more woodland. Descend the slope, ignoring the track to the left that leads to some derelict buildings, and instead take the raised path that runs along the left side of the dry, grassy floor of a millpond. Carry on along the path where it descends steps to a footbridge over Cam Brook.

Climb the stile at the end of the bridge and go straight up the slope and on over the pasture to the stile to the right of the gate. Then walk ahead to pass to the left of Marl House farm, where a waymark directs you along the farm track. Go on to pass some outbuildings, turn sharp left immediately beyond the last barn and descend a sunken track. Turn left again to pass in front of a small house, Hawthornthwaite, and take a small gate up against the end wall of the house. Walk on to pass through a gateless gap and continue to a stile to the left of a gate. Carry on down beside a hollow to your right and then a fenced plantation, also to your right.

At the foot of the pasture climb the stile in the corner into Hinberry Wood. Follow the little path under huge Scots pines, bear left at the waymark and descend steps down the steep woodland. At the bottom of the steps turn right, cross a footbridge and continue along through the trees on a level path, which soon becomes flagged, to join a road. Turn left to cross the Marshaw Wyre and continue to the parking area.

# WALK 13

## Tarnbrook and Marshaw Wyre

| | |
|---|---|
| **Distance** | 9.5km (6 miles) |
| **Time** | 3–4 hours |
| **Terrain** | Easy walking for most of the way; can be muddy after heavy rain |
| **Maps** | OS Explorer OL41 |

The two sources of the River Wyre rise in the Forest of Bowland at Tarnbrook Fell and Marshaw Fell. Called the Tarnbrook Wyre and the Marshaw Wyre, these two lovely becks come together at Abbeystead Reservoir, into which they flow. Then as the River Wyre they flow south, meeting with the River Calder downstream of Garstang and the River Brock near the village of St Michael's on Wyre. The river then takes a course west over the Fylde Plain before finally turning north to flow between Fleetwood and Knott End into the Irish Sea at Morecambe Bay.

This walk takes you beside both the Marshaw and the Tarnbrook, and skirts the rolling moors on the way.

Park as for walk 12, Abbeystead and Dolphinholme, at Stoops Bridge beside the Marshaw Wyre at Abbeystead, grid ref 563544. Cross the lane beside which you have parked and go through a gate to begin the well-waymarked and signposted route across a large pasture. In spring the deciduous woodland on either side is full of birdsong. Continue ahead to the far right corner to take a gate to the left of a shed. Look left to see Abbeystead, the magnificent mansion of the Duke of Westminster, who owns all the land over which this walk passes. With tongue in cheek, a local described it as the duke's country cottage.

Cross the wooden footbridge over the Marshaw Wyre and continue ahead with the hurrying water to your left.

To your right there is a pasture with woodland away beyond, and as you climb gently you have a sudden pleasing glimpse of Hawthornthwaite Fell. Look for waymarks on the fence beside a small copse which now lies between you and the Marshaw. Pause at the next kissing gate and look down into a dark hollow where the river makes a sharp loop.

Go through a gate into more woodland and look for a stone marker telling you that the trees were planted in 1908, when Lord Sefton was the owner of Abbeystead. Beyond the next stile descend steepish steps to cross a small stream. The path then skirts left of a grassy bluff to come close to the lively brook once more. Continue straight ahead, where the Marshaw makes another large loop, and cross a footbridge hidden until the last moment by bushes of gorse. Here is a sheltered corner to linger awhile.

Go through the kissing gate beyond the bridge and climb the slope. Walk ahead to an easy-to-miss stile in the far corner, the river immediately to your right, and continue along the pleasing way. Ignore a small gate on your right

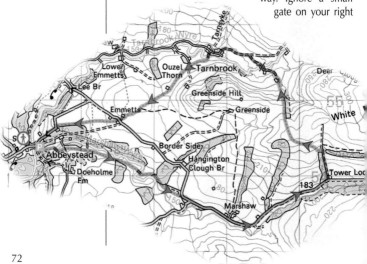

The Marshaw Wyre

and continue on to cross another footbridge over a tiny stream tumbling through more fine woodland. Climb steadily, woodland to your left and dark moorland slopes beyond the pastures to your right. Where the wood turns away left, go ahead, soon to walk beside a fence on your right. Climb the stile at the end of the fence to join a road.

Stroll on along the beech-lined road, making full use of the verge. At the end of the trees take a stile over the wall on the right – topped with a white waymark, it is a permissive route. Continue on, keeping parallel with the wall by the road, to pass the tiny settlement of Marshaw. Carry on until you can take a ladderstile over a boundary wall and rejoin the road.

Press on, again making full use of the verge, with the river beside you dancing between oaks and pines. Once past a footbridge that leads into an 'open access' area you can see, on the other side of the road, attractive Tower Lodge. Cross, and just before the dwelling take a gate onto a gravel track.

Ascend the stony way into the high pastures above the valley of the Marshaw to come to a three-armed sign-

*Pretty Tower Lodge*

post. Here leave the track and, once over a gully,

continue right to pass through a gap in a ruined wall. Go on ascending half right until you come to a boundary wall running from the brow of the pasture right down into the valley. Take a stepped gap stile through the wall above a gate to your left.

From here you can see the next stile across a smaller pasture – it is reached along a rather wet path. Walk ahead to the next ladderstile, a metal one. From here you have a good view of Dunkenhaw Fell, sloping upwards, bleak and harsh, towards Ward's Stone.

Beyond the metal ladderstile turn right and drop down the slope. Ignore the stile on the right and carry on down to pass through a waymarked gate. From here you can see Morecambe Bay, silvery blue, stretching away westwards. Head on down the pasture, with magnificent beeches over the wall on the right, to a step stile in the corner of two walls. Descend a little and then look over the wall on the right to see the immensely deep trench of Spreight Clough. To continue, step over a gully on your left and then descend the glorious way to pass through the left of two gates. Go on through the next gate, giving access to a farm track that crosses a yard between two barns. Cross a small stone bridge and take the track towards Gilberton farm. Follow the clear waymarks to wind right before the dwelling and cross the Tarnbrook Wyre by a footbridge on the right.

Beyond, walk the farm access track until it passes through a waymarked wall on the right and joins a wider track, along which you continue. Stride on until you come to a gate that allows you to walk between the little cluster of houses at Tarnbrook (a dead end for cars). Once there were 25 dwellings here and the people made felt hats and gloves. When you reach the little green take the signposted track leading left. This brings you to a footbridge over the Tarnbrook Wyre.

Stride uphill along a grassy track and then take the step stile in the wall to the right of the gate at the end of the track. Go ahead to a waymarked stile, and then head slightly left across the next pasture to a ladderstile almost obscured by a bush. Cross the farm track and take the stile opposite. Stroll on, the fence to your left, to a stone stile in the left corner. Carry on, passing a barn on your right, and follow the arrow directing you ahead to a ladderstile. Beyond, step over a muddy stream into rough pasture. Press on with the fence to your right, and where it swings right go ahead across a large pasture. The next stile is in the left corner of a pasture by a fence, beyond a wet patch.

Turn left and walk to the next ladderstile. Beyond, turn right and walk beside the hedge to the ladderstile onto the access track to Top of Emmetts farm. Turn left, walk to the road and cross. Beyond the waymarked stile bear right towards a waymarked telegraph pole. Keep ahead with a fence, a ditch and an ancient bank-wall to the right and climb the stile in the corner of the pasture. Go ahead at the cross of tracks and carry on across a long pasture with woodland to your left. Take the ladderstile in the left corner into the garden of a cottage. Walk to the road, turn left and descend the hill, with a pleasant glimpse of the reservoir through the trees. Pass the lodge to Abbeystead and continue to the parking area at Stoops Bridge.

# WALK 14

## Clougha Pike

| | |
|---|---|
| **Distance** | 9.4km (5¾ miles) |
| **Time** | 3–4 hours |
| **Terrain** | Moorland tracks, some distinct, but parts of others not always visible; some boggy walking, particularly after a spell of wet weather; lower-level part of the route is a pleasure to walk and well waymarked |
| **Maps** | OS Explorer OL41 |

Park in the large car park opposite the Jubilee Tower, grid ref 543574, on the Quernmore road through the Trough of Bowland. Leave by a narrow grassy path leading from the

Clougha Pike (413m (1356ft)) stands above the Forest of Bowland and the views from the summit are superb. You can see the Bowland fells, Blackpool Tower, the Lakeland fells, Lancaster, Morecambe Bay and the three peaks – Whernside, Ingleborough and Penyghent. The trig point on the top of the pike has been painted white, and during much of this walk you can see it clearly across the moorland and from over the pastures below.

The walk starts from the Jubilee Tower, built to commemorate Queen Victoria's golden jubilee.

back of the car park, descend a slope to step over a stream and continue ahead, keeping parallel with the fence to your right. The indistinct path, which has been well walked, wanders up the steepish moorland slope, winding round wet areas and crossing ditches and small streams.

The vegetation of the unfenced moorland to your left is composed of matt grass, square rush, deer grass and cotton grass, and is in great contrast to the vast area of moorland on the other side of the fence. Here sheep have been kept out and huge cushions of heather stretch for as

*Jubilee Tower*

far as the eye can see. This side of the fence is greatly 'preferred' by the many grouse that are found here.

Follow the fence up for about 2.3km (just under 1½ miles) to reach a stile at the fence corner. Climb this and walk southeast along a much better path, which you are asked not to stray from. A short distance along you reach the cairn on Grit Fell. From here you can look ahead over the lonely rolling moorland to Ward's Stone, and see in the distance to your left the three peaks.

Return to cross the stile once more and walk on ahead with another fence to your right. The path is easy to spot but rough to walk. Continue to a stile just to the left of the fence corner then go through more heather. Where the route gets boggy the path becomes indistinct.

*The white trig point is topped with a viewfinder that names the fells you can see, and gathered around the trig point are several stone shelters.*

Choose the driest way and walk towards a large cairn, clearly seen ahead over more bog. Soon the path becomes much easier to follow and there are magnificent views to pause and enjoy.

Go past the cairn and on to the next one. Now the path improves and becomes distinct as you bear slightly left towards Clougha Pike. Go on over the stony plateau to arrive at the summit. ◀

Leave the top by a good path that descends south-east. For a few steps it keeps in line with some old fence posts on the left, and parallel with the path you followed to reach the trig point, then slants easily down the escarpment.

From now on the way is much drier to walk. At an indistinct Y-junction take the right branch, keeping parallel with but some distance from a derelict wall on the right. Look far left to spot the Jubilee Tower.

Carry on down the enjoyable path – such a contrast to the earlier ones – over the open pasture, then step across rush-lined Rowton Brook. Go on through a series of gates between pastures alongside the deepish valley of the brook. When you have to choose between two gates, take the one on the right and press on down the continuing track to another gate. Walk ahead over more open pasture towards Rooten Brook Farm, keeping beside a boundary wall to the left. Cross the turf bridge over the brook and go on through a gate into the farmyard.

Bear left and head on for a dozen or so steps. At the end of the barn on your right, turn left to strike across the pasture to a stone footbridge over the brook again. Climb the ladderstile beyond and venture on, half right, to another obvious ladderstile. Turn left and pass through a gate, then walk in front of the farmhouse. Wind round right beside it to pass through a gate and on over a step stile into a pasture.

Stroll ahead through several stiles between pastures until you reach a marker post directing you half right to a stile onto a road called Quernmore Brow. Cross and walk right for just over 90 metres to turn left onto a concrete access track. After about 200 metres take the waymarked step stile into a pasture. Head up the pasture and at a fence corner go on over the pasture, keeping the fence to your right. Very soon the pasture becomes fenced on your left, with a row of hawthorns beside the fence. You are in fact walking a long, narrow, fenced field.

Climb the stile to the left of a gate to join a narrow road and walk right to pass through the tiny hamlet of

Hare Appletree. Go on through a gate and ford the stream ahead. Turn right as directed by the waymark, and when you reach the end of a barn wind round left of a huge slurry tank – as best you can – and climb the slope on the left to an obvious stile into a pasture.

Head towards a prominent waymark standing in the middle of the pasture. From here walk on to the edge of a stream, keeping well to the left of a shelter belt of Scots pine. Descend the slope, jump across the stream and climb up the other side. Continue ahead to negotiate two more little gutters and then stroll on, keeping left of a hillock, with open moorland to the left. From here you have a good view of the white trig point on Clougha Pike.

Head towards a step stile over the wall in the left corner of the pasture. Beyond, go on over a succession of stiles between pastures until the last stile brings you to a concrete track. Walk left up the track to pass in front of Westfield House farm and then go on up the tarmacked access drive to reach the Jubilee Tower once more. Perhaps you will still have enough energy to climb to the top to enjoy the superb view.

*Clougha Pike viewed after descent*

# WALK 15

## *Ward's Stone, Bowland*

| | |
|---|---|
| **Distance** | 19km (12 miles) |
| **Time** | 5 hours |
| **Terrain** | A gravelled shooters' track takes you up to the ridge and another brings you down – rough peaty paths, which can be soggy after rain, take you over the extensive ridge that links these tracks; there is also a virtually traffic-free lane to walk |
| **Maps** | OS Explorer OL41 |

Ward's Stone (561m (1848ft)) is the highest hill in the Forest of Bowland and stands guardian over the city of Lancaster and Morecambe Bay. Much of the route is not a right of way but follows concessionary paths that cross the grouse moors of the Duke of Westminster, and these can be closed occasionally during the shooting season [dates, please].

The broad plateau is named Ward's Stone and it has two trig points. One is at the eastern edge (561m (1848ft)), where there are fascinating rock formations, and the other is at the western edge, with even more spectacular rocks. The rocks at the western edge are also called Ward's Stone (560m (1845ft)) and the whole plateau is named after these rocks. The views from the plateau are superb. You can look into Yorkshire to see Ingleborough and Penyghent, and also across Morecambe Bay to the Lakeland fells.

This is the longest walk in the book and is suitable only for experienced fell walkers. It is a good-weather walk and should be undertaken only when there are enough hours of daylight to complete the route safely. There are no useful escape routes, so if the weather deteriorates, turn back. No dogs, no camping and no fires are allowed on the hill. It is an exciting walk, and when completed gives you a great sense of achievement.

Park in the small car park, grid ref 563544, at Stoops Bridge, Abbeystead (see walk 12, Abbeystead to Dolphinholme). Return to the Abbeystead road and turn

left to cross the bridge over the Tarnbrook Wyre. A few metres along take the way-marked footpath on the right side of the road and walk ahead along a good track through gracious parkland.

As you near the road at Lower Lee, walk towards the right corner of the pasture and cross a footbridge and then a stile onto the narrow road. Turn right.

Continue on to a junction where you take the narrow lane signposted 'Tarnbrook and cul-de-sac'. Walk on, soon to come beside the Tarnbrook Wyre hurrying over its stony bed, and in summer through lush vegetation.

Carry on for 2km (1¼ miles) to the hamlet of Tarnbrook. Here you pass between some pretty dwellings, go by the tiny village green, then follow the way, now a track, through a gate out onto low moorland.

Ignore the way-marked right turn that leads to Gilberton farm and stroll on until the now gravelled track winds left and begins to climb up through bracken and then heather and bilberry. Go on up the well-graded way with the grassy slopes of Wolfhole Crag, which supports a small plantation of Scots pine, to your right. The bouldery edge of Tarnbrook Fell towers on the left. Continue upwards, remaining on the track as it teeters along the edge of Gables Clough and then winds some more before descending to a footbridge. Below flows the Wyre, having gathered water from the slopes above. Climb the slope beyond and follow the track as it levels out and finally comes to the ridge at Brown Syke.

Do not pass through the gateless gap in the fence and wall ahead, but turn left and walk on with the boundary to your right. At first there are large areas of exposed peat and gullies of peat, which make for difficult walking after rain, but keep along the little path beside the fence and walk where others have marked out the way with their bootprints. The path eventually improves and you should remain faithfully on the left side of the newish stretches of wall or the elderly fence. Pause regularly to enjoy the views into Yorkshire.

Then the fence climbs fairly steeply and there are several peaty hollows to negotiate. Where the fence turns away a narrow, indistinct path leads up to the open

83

moorland to the eastern edge of Ward's Stone. Here there is a striking rock feature whose parts are named on the map as Grey Mare with Foal and Queen's Chair. Just beyond these is a commemorative trig point.

From this spot a dry narrow path leads on along the ridge to arrive at the western edge of the plateau, where there is a large collection of contorted boulders. Another trig point graces the little hillock, and close by is the huge boulder that gives its name to the hill, Ward's Stone. Locate the little path that carries on in a westerly direction and begin your descent off the plateau on a rough peaty way. This leads down to Cabin Flat, an extensive area of peaty moorland. The little path passes through heather, climbs up and down small peaty gullies, and sometimes seems to disappear in mire. Pick your way carefully and head on. Pass two small pools of water on your left, and when you can see the noticeboards beside the track you need for your descent, the path disappears. Pick your way carefully through the heather to join the track where a notice tells you about the 'Access strip' – a narrow strip across the moor from which you must not stray – and waymarks direct you on your way.

*Looking up to the Bowland Fells*

84

Turn left to go down the gravelled track, with a deep clough (narrow gorge) to your left, and also pass the shooters' luncheon huts. Ignore a track going off left and carry on down and down, eventually to pass through pleasing pastures. As you near Higher Lee the track winds right to pass in front of the house. Follow the waymark directing you left and turn left at the road.

Descend the short hill and go through a gate on the right. This gives onto the end of the track you took almost at the outset of the walk. Head on along the track with fine deciduous woodland all around – a great contrast after the treeless tops. Continue to the stile onto the road, turn left, cross Stoops Bridge and then go right into the parking area.

*The Grey Mare and Foal, and Queen's Chair, Ward's Stone*

# WALK 16

## *Slaidburn*

| | |
|---|---|
| **Distance** | 11.4km (7 miles) |
| **Time** | 4 hours |
| **Terrain** | Easy walking all the way |
| **Maps** | OS Explorer OL41 |

Slaidburn lies in the eastern corner of the Forest of Bowland. It is a village in which to linger to view its Wesleyan Chapel (1889), fine war memorial, cobbled pavements, charming St Andrew's Church with its box pews and three-tiered pulpit, and its famous inn, the Hark to Bounty. Until 1875 it was called the Dog Inn, but 'Hark to Bounty' was the comment of a squire who visited the inn that year and heard his favourite hound, Bounty, barking.

*Hark to Bounty Inn, Slaidburn*

Park in the public car park, grid ref 714523, close by the bridge over the River Hodder at Slaidburn (there are toilets here). From here turn right, and with the long green that edges the River Hodder on your left, walk through the lovely village. Where the road swings left towards Newton, continue straight ahead to walk in front of the inn.

Continue along Back Lane, with sturdy stone houses on either side, until you have passed Slaidburn's medical centre, then take the signposted footpath to the right into woodland. Walk through the trees to the side of Croasdale Brook, where in spring ramsons carpet the woodland floor.

Climb the stile, continue upstream, then take the next stile into a pasture and continue ahead beside a young hedge on your right. Continue gently downhill to climb a ladderstile in a short stretch of wall. Go on with the river

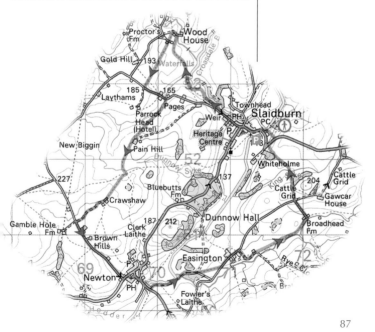

on the right, keeping to the right of Tenter Hill, a large grassy hummock. Ascend the stone stile over the wall beyond and use the large stone slab to step across a small stream. Follow the path to the far left corner of the next pasture, stroll left at the wall and continue to where the path winds right and soon becomes part of a walled track to Myttons, a farmhouse built in 1846. Go through the waymarked gate into its large yard – ahead is a craft shop.

Follow the farm's access track as it winds round to the left. Ignore an arrowed way right and go on up the track to pass a Dutch barn. Just beyond, on the left, climb a stile by a gate. Walk ahead for a short distance to go through another gate and continue on with the wall to your right. Enjoy the utter peace of this lovely area – no traffic or aircraft noise, just the twitter of meadow pipits and the song of the skylark. Follow the wall as it winds a short way left to a waymark and then turns right. Continue with it still beside you on the right to climb a rather awkward stile in the wall corner. Straddle the stone step stile ahead and then walk on to a signposted stile onto a road. Turn left and walk on to pass Ellerbeck Hall, dated 1694. This grand house with stone-mullioned windows sits in a sunny hollow surrounded by rolling pastures.

Continue down the lane to cross a small bridge over Eller Beck and turn right along a signposted track to a gate. Walk ahead along the track to a stile into a fenced area, pass between two ponds, and go on to climb a stone stepped stile. Walk on beside a thorn hedge on the left until you reach Pain Hill, a farmhouse dated 1689. Keep to the right of all the farm outbuildings to go through a wall stile onto the farm access track. Turn right and then almost immediately left to hug the side of a walled sycamore wood on the left (it has a rookery). Climb a stone stile and continue along the track over pastures. Where the track ceases, stroll on parallel with a wall to your left and then a beech wood beyond the wall. Take a stile into a paddock and go ahead on the waymarked farm track, ignoring an arrowed way on the left, and walk past Crawshaw farm. Stride on along the farm track to the road.

Turn left and descend the pleasing hedged lane to reach Newton's Quaker Burial Ground on the right. ▶ Then continue to the village of Newton with its fine 16th- and 17th-century houses.

At the T-junction bear left, and at the Y-junction take the right branch to come to the tiny green with its seemingly over-large signpost. Here descend right to pass charming Newton Hall on your left, and on to fine Newton Bridge over the River Hodder. Turn left on the far side of the bridge to go through an unsignposted stile. Wind round beside the hurrying river to go through a gate, and continue upstream on a delightful footpath. Where the river turns away left, continue ahead along a footpath to pass through a gate. Ignore the ladderstile immediately on your left and walk ahead to cross a footbridge over a tributary stream. Wind round right beside fenced woodland on your right, and at the corner strike diagonally across the pasture. A gate in the top right corner gives onto a narrow lane.

Turn left and stride on to pass Robinsons Farm (dated 1699) and Timothy's Cottage. Ignore the footpath on the right and continue along the lane to reach the Manor House with stone-mullioned windows at Easington. Take

You might like to pause in the walled enclosure – there is a seat here to allow you to enjoy this quiet corner. (Notice the several headstones, all exactly the same.)

*Newton Bridge*

the signposted right turn immediately after the last barn. Walk ahead between the farm buildings and on down a track to join another track where you turn left. Follow this track as it leads to a tractor bridge over Easington Brook. Do NOT cross the bridge, but take the stile on the left to continue along the side of the fenced stream. Here you might see oystercatchers snoozing on a pebbly reach.

Just before a fenced enclosure of newly planted trees wind left to walk round the edge of the plantation and pass through a gate. (Do not go *through* the plantation because at the time of writing there are some very boggy pools that must be avoided.) Continue ahead over a pasture to Broadhead Farm. Go through a gate and through the farm outbuildings to join the farm access track. Turn left to rejoin the narrow lane, which you cross, and then climb the signposted gate opposite. Walk up the slope keeping the boundary to the left. Go through a gate on the left, just before a larch plantation, turn right and continue down beside the woodland.

At the bottom of the slope climb the stepped stile, and then turn left to climb uphill and on, close beside a walled copse. Follow the grassy trod as it swings right downhill to a gate onto the road. Turn right, and after a few steps cross with care to go through another gate. Beyond, follow an indistinct path which drops downhill. At its foot walk left along a short track to join the road at the bottom of its hairpin bend. Turn right to cross the bridge over the River Hodder and the car park lies beyond on the right.

# WALK 17

## *Bolton-by-Bowland*

| | |
|---|---|
| **Distance** | Walk 1: 5km (3 miles) |
| | Walk 2: 7.4km (4½ miles) |
| **Time** | First part of the walk 2 hours |
| | Second part of the walk 3 hours |
| **Terrain** | Easy walking all the way |
| **Maps** | OS Explorer OL41 |

Stroll the glorious countryside that surrounds tranquil Bolton-by-Bowland to enjoy a quietness that is broken only by birdsong. The village has two greens. On the smaller of these stand the stump of an old market cross, a millstone and some ancient stocks. The charming Church of St Peter and St Paul, with its magnificent tower, stands on the left a short distance along the Gisburn Road. Inside the walls are of unrendered stone and the pews of oak. In the small chapel look for the memorial slab to Sir Ralph Pudsay, who rebuilt the church in the 15th century. Here, carved in stone, you can see Ralph, his three wives and his 25 children. Beyond the church and overlooking the second green is the fine old courthouse with its splendid weather vane.

This walk can be completed as one, in a figure-of-eight, or it can be done in two separate parts with a break for lunch in the attractive village.

Park in the car park, grid ref 785494, on the east side of Skirden Bridge at the west end of Bolton-by-Bowland. It is signed Recycling Centre and there are toilets here.

### Walk 1

Turn right out of the parking area and walk on to reach the church. Opposite the church take King Henry Mews, a signposted metalled way leading towards Bolton Hall Farm. It once led to now- demolished Bolton Hall, home of Sir Ralph Pudsay.

Walk the long tree-lined avenue, climbing gently through pleasing parkland. Continue past the remains of an ancient cross on the left and stroll on to a Y-junction. Ignore the entrance to the dwelling and take the left branch. After a few steps take the track on the left leading to a stile. Ascend gently beyond, passing a large pond on the right, and go uphill and through a gateless gap. Go on ahead, and beyond the next stile carry on to the side

*The Church of St Peter and St Paul at Bolton-by-Bowland*

of deciduous woodland. Turn right and continue with the trees to your left. Ignore the stile in the wall on your right, and keep going to climb stone steps over a wall to the right of a farm gate. To the right again stands Pendle Hill, a benevolent giant in sunshine.

Wind left on a track beyond the gate, and in a few steps go right as directed by a waymark to pass between the two dwellings at Scott Laithe. Walk on through outbuildings to the next waymark, directing you left beyond a small stone building. Then turn right to stroll along a narrow path beside barns and parked vehicles on the right. Go over a series of well-arrowed and -constructed stiles, the last of which gives access to a pasture where you descend diagonally to a stile in the far right corner. Beyond, descend a little more to take another stile to continue below the ash, oak and elm that clothe the steep bank sloping down to the River Ribble far below.

Continue ahead along an old sunken grassy way with thorn bushes to the right. Just before the farm buildings at Foden, take a sturdy stile on the right to wind round a barn and then go on to the next stile to reach the farm's access track. Wind left along the track and past a pretty house to go through a waymarked gate. Bear half right over a pasture to walk beside a hedge on the right and continue up to a ladderstile in the corner. Beyond, go ahead in the same general direction to climb a further stile. Next, press on to pass to the right of a row of oaks and come to a kissing gate giving onto the road to Gisburn. Turn left and descend the hedged way into Bolton-by-Bowland. If you were unable to visit the church on your outward route you might like to go up the steps on the right leading to a path to the huge oak door into the building. Then continue to the car park.

**Walk 2**
Turn left out of the car park to cross the bridge over Skirden Beck and take the access track on the left. Where the track swings left, take the well-signposted stile ahead. Beyond, take the signposted stile on the right and carry

*Bridge over Holden Beck, Bolton-by-Bowland*

on along the waymarked route, with the fence to the left, and climb the step stile in the corner. Carry on ahead with the wall to the left, then go beside some sheds and through gates to join the road. Cross the road, climb the step stile opposite and walk ahead over the pasture. Ignore the step stile on the right and take the steps over the wall ahead. Walk round the boundary of a dwelling to take a stile tucked in the corner among bushes. Turn right to take a step stile through the wall, and head on with the wall of the houses to your right to climb a step stile onto the road.

Turn left and walk for a few steps to a crossroads in the hamlet of Holden. Here turn left in the direction of Lane Ends. Walk on to cross the bridge over Holden Beck and then turn left into the waymarked track. Ignore the footpath to the left and carry on up the drive of a dwelling. Just before the house take the grassy track that runs to the right and go through a gate into a pasture. Climb the next stile and then the next one onto a narrow track.

Cross the track and go over the stile opposite to ascend the large pasture, drifting slightly to the left to go through a large gate gap in a hedge, and continuing with a hedge to your right. Keep on the same diagonal to a difficult-to-spot small gate in the hedge near the top left corner. Beyond, go over the stile immediately ahead. Keep climbing to go through a gate, and then on and up through a gated step at the top of the slope to the left of a barn called Lower Laithe.

Next, swing right and uphill to steps over a wall and turn left to walk behind (right) Higher Heights farm. Follow the waymark directing you ahead to the gate at the end of the track, avoiding all other gates. Once out into the high open pasture enjoy the extensive views over this remote corner of Lancashire. Then head gently downhill to the far left corner and go over one stile, and then another immediately right, and into a rough pasture.

Walk on beside the fence on your left, go through a gate and then wind round left. Ignore the stile on your left and begin your descent of a wide sunken track called Rodhill Lane. ▶ Go on down the long track to come to two dwellings on the left, Rodhill Gate and Rodhill farm.

Wind left round the dwellings and then head diagonally right over the sloping pasture in the direction of Hague farm. At the corner of two hedges go over a stile and onto a ditch. Bear right beside the ditch until you can join an access track, left, to the farmhouse and outbuildings. Continue through the latter until you are able to descend, right, to open pasture where you stride across to a footbridge over Hell Syke. Head on to a stile giving onto the road, cross over and continue down a track to another fine footbridge over Holden Beck once more.

Continue along a rather indistinct path to come to the side of woodland on your right, with Skirden Beck also to your right, to come to a stile at the corner of the wood. Strike on ahead to cross a hidden stile in the hedge, and then climb gently through the lovely parkland before descending to the stile onto the lane taken at the outset of the walk. Return along the lane and turn right to rejoin the car park.

At the time of writing the track was being improved – it was newly fenced and gates were in place, but still rather wet and rough underfoot.

# WALK 18

## *Dunsop Bridge, Bowland*

| | |
|---|---|
| **Distance** | 13km (8 miles) |
| **Time** | 4 hours |
| **Terrain** | Some wild open moorland that can be quite boggy after rain; some 'dead-end' road walking |
| **Maps** | OS Explorer OL41 |

The village of Dunsop Bridge is built around the picturesque humpbacked bridge over the River Dunsop. It is the gateway to the magnificent Trough of Bowland, a beautiful, lonely upland area. It is also very nearly the centre of Britain. The actual spot, as calculated by Ordnance Survey, is grid ref 637565, 600 metres west of Whitendale Hanging Stones. Dunsop Bridge is the nearest village to this central point, a fact recognised in 1992 when the explorer Sir Ranulph Fiennes unveiled BT's 100,000th payphone on the village green.

This is a great walk for those who like quiet pastures, the habitat of ground-nesting birds, and lonely moors where grouse call from acres of heather. It should be undertaken in good weather – not after heavy rain or when the tops are covered in mist.

Park at Dunsop Bridge car park, grid ref 661550, and turn right out of the car park to walk with the green to your left and the River Dunsop beyond. Pass the garage, once a blacksmith's forge and the hub of the village, and continue past the post office to turn right just before the famous bridge. Walk the private road that continues beside the pretty river to your left, with birch and conifer to your right. Once across meadows, go past several cottages and on along a good track, following the arrowed way. To the right, steep slopes support ash, below which, in spring, is a wonderful carpet of bluebells. Cross the fine footbridge over the Dunsop and turn right to continue with the river now to your right. You should be able to spot several dippers here. On either side huge forests of conifers begin to crowd in on the valley.

Proceed through the austere valley, where the dark green of sitka spruce is lightened with areas of larch. Continue past waterboard buildings, small dams, flood barriers, a footbridge, and a huge water pipe that carries water from Thirlmere in the Lake District to Preston, Blackburn and Blackpool.

Do not cross the bridge here, but continue for a few metres to go over a fine wooden footbridge. Once on the far side of the River Dunsop, turn left to walk a good track with grass down the middle. To your left is Whitendale River, hurrying below a gritstone cliff where oak and ash thrive. To your right heather banks stretch up to the blanket of conifers. Carry on where the path winds right into a clough (a narrow ravine). Watch for the place where walkers use stones to ford the tiny stream descending through Little Costy Clough. Head across the tiny triangle of ground to cross a plank bridge (with a non-slip surface) over the stream tumbling down Costy Clough.

Ascend towards a small footbridge and turn left before it to walk a pleasing buttressed path edged with heather, bilberry and rowan. This path brings you once again to the side of and well above the narrow Whitendale River. Carry on the clear level path through carpets of heather towards Whitendale farm, nestling in its moorland hollow. On reaching the track to the farm, turn left and go on through two gates to descend to the left of the buildings and join the valley road.

Turn right and then almost immediately left to take the indistinct but well-signposted path up the steepish northern slopes of Middle Knoll. When you reach the first waymark the path becomes distinct. Pause here to look back down to the lonely farm below and then walk on up the waymarked path to a gate in the fell wall. Beyond, bear slightly left, faithfully following the waymarks across the moorland – use clumps of rushes to cross the wettest areas. Cross a shallow clough and go on, keeping to the left of a small tarn. Beyond, in the corner of the pasture is the waymarked stile over a wall, which you climb. ◀

*If you followed the wall, heading north, you would reach the Whitendale Hanging Stones and be 600 metres east of the centre of Britain.*

Continue ahead with a wall to your right to another waymarked stile in the right corner of the pasture. Beyond, an arrow directs you left along a farm track. Keep to this track and press on where it turns sharp right to begin its descent towards Brennand Farm, hidden in the folds of the fell. As the farm comes into view, and at the point where the very rough track swings right, turn left to take a footpath that runs above the Brennand River, lying below to your right. (There is a good view across to the

*Valley of the River Dunsop, Bowland*

farm.) Follow the easy way that traverses the slopes and joins the valley road just beyond Lower Brennand farm.

Stroll on along the road and take the right fork at the Y-junction to descend to join your outward route, passing the waterboard buildings again. Carry on down the valley until you reach the wooden bridge crossed early on in the walk. Go over, stride on past the houses and keep straight across the meadows back to Dunsop Bridge.

*View from the slopes of Middle Knoll, Dunsop Bridge*

# WALK 19

## *Whitewell, Bowland*

| | |
|---|---|
| **Distance** | 9.8km (6 miles) |
| **Time** | 3–4 hours |
| **Terrain** | Generally easy walking, but there are two rough areas that require careful navigating: the pastures from Ing Wood to the access track to Stakes, and the short awkward patch just before Higher Lees |
| **Maps** | OS Explorer OL41 |

This walk starts very close to the Inn at Whitewell. The proprietor is Richard Bowman who, as his name suggests, is descended from an archer – one of those who helped to beat the French at the Battle of Agincourt. The bows used in the battle were made from trees in the forest around Whitewell. In 1380 the Keeper of the King's Forest lived at what is now the inn. The chapel beside the parking area was established in about 1400.

A 17th-century house called Stakes stands by the River Hodder with a sturdy row of stepping stones across the water. Locally these are called 'hipping stones' and there is a right of way across them – when they stand above the surging river! The farm belongs to the Duchy of Lancaster. Look for the Latin words about the unpredictability of life inscribed over a doorway to this very pleasing, much-mullioned late-Stuart farmhouse.

*The Inn at Whitewell, Bowland*

From the car park below St Michael's Church at Whitewell, grid ref 658468, walk back to the road and with the inn to your left climb the road opposite. A few steps along the road brings you to a footpath sign on the right. Climb stone steps to enter a pasture and walk ahead over wet ground to join a track. Bear right to pass to the right of a house and continue slightly right along a good track. It is worth several pauses to look back on the wonderful view of the Hodder valley.

Follow the track as it climbs a sloping pasture. Ignore the gate in the wall ahead and bear left to take another gate in the top wall. Walk right alongside the wall to your right to pass through a fine wrought-iron deer-proof kissing gate. Stroll on to climb a stile, go on through the next gate and carry on to another tall kissing gate. Beyond, bear right down a track almost to the road and, remaining within the pasture, continue to the signposted gate ahead. This gives access to the road. Cross the road and walk on to take a stile on the right at the corner of woodland.

Strike diagonally across the pasture and walk along the outside of Ing Wood to a stile. Beyond, go ahead to the left of a limestone outcrop and then gradually descend to join a track, ignoring all stiles through the fence to the river bank. Step across two little streams, close together and marked as 'fords' on the map. Pass through a waymarked gate to a stile. Beyond, bear steadily half left uphill over rough pathless ground. Cross another ford to go on to a signposted gate onto a farm track.

Turn right to descend to Stakes farm, standing solidly beside the River Hodder. You might like to spend some time in this lovely spot before returning up the lane to the signpost and going through the gate. Continue ahead beside the fence on your right. Cross a small stream and bear slightly left to climb the stile in the fence ahead, then carry on to join the access track to Lower Lees farm.

Walk right, away from the farmhouse, and where the track soon turns right, leave it to go through a gate and continue ahead towards Lower Lees cottage. Wind right round its garden to stride on to more stiles in and then out of a narrow copse. Stride ahead to a clear waymark and follow the diversion right, thus avoiding the house named Middle Lees on the map.

*Hipping stones at Stakes farm*

Cross the road and walk on along the road opposite to a signposted footpath on the left, just beyond a copse. Drop down the slope to cross a footbridge, then turn right and walk upstream to the next stile. Go on beyond, watching out for the next stile in the hedge on your right – it is marked with a large white disk. Once over the stile the right of way is difficult to follow. Look for large yellow disks up in the trees to help you through the very rough pathless copse (cattle have poached the ground here). Descend the banking of the narrow stream with care and step across the water. Then walk on for a short distance to re-cross the stream. Continue up the pasture, away from the stream, to arrive at a gate on the right giving onto a track just before Higher Lees farmhouse.

Go on in front of the dwelling and stride ahead along the continuing track. Look for the gap stile in the electric fence (if it is in place) and then walk ahead to a stile. Beyond, climb steadily half left to a stile in the wall up against a plantation. This allows you to follow the wall, left, around the outside of the woodland until you reach the next boundary wall. Here head left again towards fine Radholme Laund farmhouse.

Pass through a waymarked gate in the wall to the left of the dwelling, and stride through a yard to a gate onto open pasture. Continue uphill beside the wall to the top corner of the pasture to go through another grand kissing gate. Cut across the corner to take another and then begin your descent, remaining by the wall on your left. Go through a gate and continue descending to a stile through the next wall. Drop down to pass in front of the house, passed on the other side at the outset of the walk. Strike across the pasture to the gate and steps taken earlier, and then turn left to descend to the car park.

# WALK 20

## *Garstang and Nicky Nook*

| | |
|---|---|
| **Distance** | 4.5km (9 miles) |
| **Time** | 5 hours |
| **Terrain** | Easy walking for most of the way; steepish descent of Nicky Nook; some walking on narrow roads |
| **Maps** | OS Explorer OL41 |

This walk starts at Garstang and explores the countryside that lies to the east of the M6 and the railway. The route crosses lush meadows full of sheep, comes beside several tranquil reservoirs, edges the lonely Bleasdale Fells and passes through deciduous woodland. Before it returns beside the River Wyre the route takes you up onto Nicky Nook, a fine rolling grassy ridge from where there are spectacular views over to the Lakeland fells and across the low-lying coastal land to Morecambe Bay.

Park in the car park between Garstang's main street and the River Wyre, grid ref 494454 (there are toilets here). Walk out of the back of the parking area to join a paved path beside the river flowing to your right. Stroll on to climb steps onto a bridge (part of a dismantled railway) to cross the hurrying water, then descend more steps to the other side of the river. Ignore a track on your left and then go down several steps to take the waymarked path on your left. Follow a distinct stiled path across pastures to a track, Lingart Lane, where you turn right. Continue on until you reach Hazelhead Lane. Turn left and stride on to pass a private access track to Higher Lingart Farm. A short distance beyond, take a signposted footpath on the right to cross the huge stepped footbridge over the railway line. Walk on to cross the high footbridge over the M6.

Go straight ahead across a meadow to climb two stiles onto Keeper's Lane. Head left along this narrow hedged lane leading into the Lancashire countryside. Ignore the first left turn and at the next T-junction turn left to walk Eidsforth Lane. Walk on to take the signposted stiled footpath on the right, opposite the end of a small plantation on your left.

Cross a footbridge on the left and then strike right to take a stiled footbridge under willows. Walk ahead along the fenced way to climb a stile, and then carry on to a stile in the right corner of the pasture. Cross a grassy track, and then go ahead to turn left in front of a barn at Burns Farm, following the waymark. Turn right and then right again out of the farmyard, and in a few steps turn left up the pleasing farm track.

Go through a gate and continue uphill along the reinforced track as it swings right to a gate and stile. Do NOT cross the stile, but turn left to go on climbing the track, with Burns Quarry Wood on the left and a fence to the right. Pause at the top of the slope to enjoy a magnificent view of the Fylde Plain to the west and ahead to the Bleasdale Fells.

Burns Quarry Wood

The track ends at two gates with a stile between them, which you climb to continue along a path to the right of a straggly thorn hedge. Descend to a pleasant little hollow where you climb another stile. Ascend the slope beyond to reach a fence where you turn right along a track to a stile. Beyond, walk left along a grassy track lined with foxgloves and willowherb in August.

Go past Moor House (dated 1866) and continue ahead along a reinforced track to pass, away to your left, Moor Farm. Carry on towards the obvious wireless station, and at a cross of tracks just before the station gate turn left to walk a grassy track. Barnacre Reservoirs soon come into view on your left. Take the right of two gates – to the east stretch the vast Bleasdale Fells. Head on past a sweet-smelling conifer plantation, alive with the calls of goldcrests and coal tits.

Follow the track as it begins to descend. A sturdy wall to your left encloses Grizedale Lea Reservoir, and far across the plain to the west you can see the white buildings of Lancaster University set in green meadows. Follow the good track to the stile to Delph Lane, where you turn left to walk for 800 metres (½ mile) along the moorland road. Cross Grizedale Bridge over Grizedale Brook and, just after, walk left along the signposted bridleway, passing through three gates.

At the signpost head right round by a turf-and-stone wall in the direction of Fell End farm, and climb steadily to a gate (muddy here) from where you can spot Black Combe beyond the Duddon Estuary. Then descend gently to climb a tied gate, and walk on to go through a waymarked wrought-iron gate in the fence on your left giving onto a good track. Descend right to the farmhouse and then bear left along the access track, ascending steadily. Where the track swings right and becomes metalled, take the gated track on the left, signposted to Grize Dale and Nicky Nook.

Go through a gate and carry on over the pastures until you can take a stile on the right. ▶ Follow the path that climbs steadily to a stone pillar – this is marked as a syphon well (for the reservoir) on the map. Continue on

If the weather is not good enough to climb Nicky Nook ignore the stile off the good track leading to the ridge and carry on along the main track through the dale.

*Trig point on Nicky Nook*

up the pathless slope to the next stone pillar. Beyond, go ahead to a good stile in the fell wall to join a distinct path climbing easily to the trig point on Nicky Nook (215m (710ft)). Here you will want to pause to enjoy the superb panoramic view.

Head back down the path until you near the stile in the wall, and bear right before it to follow an arrowed path. This leads to a steep but well-maintained descending path to the track beside Grizedale Reservoir.

Turn right along the track through the sylvan splendour, where there are pleasing glimpses through the trees of long, narrow Grizedale Reservoir. Walk on past the dam and through a gate to amble on beside the immensely steep gill. Stroll on where steep slopes sweep down to the track, and then through an open area to go through a gate with a four-armed signpost beyond. Here go ahead through a pasture, with the brook to your left, to join Higher Lane.

Walk left and carry on to pass Throstle Nest Farm on your right. Cross a ford and climb the hill to cross another (both have footbridges). Beyond, turn right to walk a track along the edge of Long Crossey Wood, with Grizedale Brook chuckling below. Beyond the next gate cross the footbridge over the motorway and follow the track as it swings left. Climb the stile and then wind right to cross the high footbridge over the railway line. Bear left to pass through the sheds of a small works to come to the corner of Hazelhead Lane. Walk right and take the second stile in the hedge on the left, just before a bridge over the brook.

Walk ahead, keeping beside the alder-lined brook on your right, to follow the path all the way to where Grizedale Brook joins the River Wyre. Amble on along the stepped and stiled way with the River Wyre, where fish jump, on your right. Go past a white bridge, built in 1927 by the Fylde Water Board to carry water from Barnacre Reservoirs to Blackpool and its surrounds, and then cross the footbridge beyond. Walk a little track to a road, turn right and immediately go through a gap on the left. Walk left to regain the path at the side of the Wyre once more, and carry on the pleasing way, passing through the Millennium Park. Go on to climb steps onto the disused railway and the bridge over the Wyre crossed earlier. Descend from the bridge and take the path also followed earlier to return to the car park.

# WALK 21

## *Garstang and Cabus Nook*

| | |
|---|---|
| **Distance** | 13km (8 miles) |
| **Time** | 4 hours |
| **Terrain** | Easy walking, although some farm tracks can be very muddy if cows are still in the pastures and returning to be milked; the towpath is a joy to walk |
| **Maps** | OS Explorer 296 |

The towpath beside the Lancaster Canal is pleasantly peaceful. At Nateby Hall Farm you leave the waterway to cross the well-drained mosses northwest of Garstang and stride the quiet Thorough Way to Cabus Nook. The route then makes an enjoyable return along the towpath once more. The canal was constructed in the late 18th century as a link between industrial centres so that heavy, bulky commodities could be delivered speedily. In 1833 horse-drawn packet boats carried passengers the 57 miles from Preston to Kendal in seven hours. Garstang is the gateway to the Forest of Bowland and is mentioned in the Domesday Book.

*Bridge over the Lancaster Canal, Garstang*

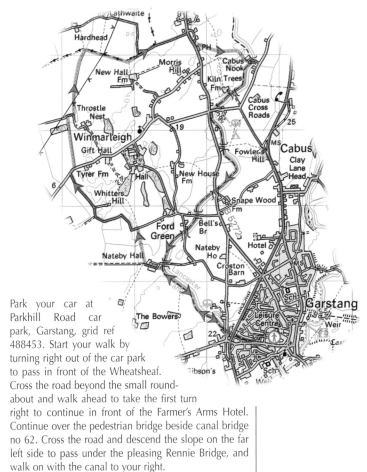

Park your car at Parkhill Road car park, Garstang, grid ref 488453. Start your walk by turning right out of the car park to pass in front of the Wheatsheaf. Cross the road beyond the small round-about and walk ahead to take the first turn right to continue in front of the Farmer's Arms Hotel. Continue over the pedestrian bridge beside canal bridge no 62. Cross the road and descend the slope on the far left side to pass under the pleasing Rennie Bridge, and walk on with the canal to your right.

Continue beneath a white bridge carrying water from Barnacre Reservoirs. Walk on under two more bridges and then out into the countryside. Carry on past Garstang Marina, where innumerable boats are tied up, and stride on until you reach some brick abutments – all that remains of bridge no 65. Before it was demolished it carried the Pilling Pig, the Garstang–Knott End railway. Stroll on to the second stile on the left, where you leave the towpath. Beyond, look left to see a well-preserved limekiln – in summer almost totally obscured by vegetation – then bear right to pass between some wartime tank traps to a gate onto a track in front of Nateby Hall farm. Turn left and follow the track between the outbuildings, continuing to a waymark pointing right just beyond a small clump of trees 50 metres beyond the farm.

Walk ahead with the trees to your right, and where they end bear slightly left across the pasture to a stile and then a footbridge (hidden until the last minute) over Lee Brook. Walk ahead to a stile set in a hawthorn hedge and giving onto Whitters Lane. ◄ Turn left and walk the narrow, traffic-free lane to the T-junction, then right to walk a few steps along Island Lane. Next, pass over a stile next to the huge metal gate on your left. At the time of writing this was very, very difficult to open, and you must pass through it as there is no other way to reach the footpath. Fortunately the footpath officer was intending to have it improved.

From here there is a good view of Winmarleigh Hall, standing redbricked and gracious among its deciduous woodland and once the home of the Patten family.

Once through the gate, walk on beside Lee Brook dyke to the next stile, to be found in the hedgerow close beside the ditch. Carry on to pass Old Hall Wood, edged with a row of poplars, on your left. Go through the next gate and head across a pasture to a stile in the hedgerow. Beyond, and very shortly turn right onto a lane, and where it swings right towards Throstle Nest, very shortly turn left onto a path to continue beside the dyke and on over the wide flat marshland.

After strolling the long pasture take the waymarked stile on your right. Continue past the tiny gas terminal on your left, almost obscured by trees, to reach the reinforced Thorough Way where you turn right. The route now takes you for just over 800 metres (½ mile) along this delightful hedge-lined way through quiet pastures to reach the B52772. Cross the road with care and walk right for 60 metres to the start of the car park at the Patten Arms.

Turn left into the car park as directed by the signpost and walk straight ahead to a hidden footbridge over Park

*Pastures near Winmarleigh Hall*

Lane Brook. Continue ahead to climb a stile in a new fence and then bear half right, keeping to the right of a small pool almost hidden by trees. This is one of the many water-filled marl pits from which clay was extracted for making bricks. Continue in the same general direction to a stile in a fence, and then on the same slightly right diagonal to a heavily waymarked gatepost. Beyond, continue beside the fence on your left and follow the fence round right to join a track where you turn right. Walk the sometimes-muddy gated way to Cabus Nook farm. Here the right of way passes to the right of the farm and then turns left between outbuildings. Follow the track as it swings left, and look for a small gate onto the towpath beyond the canal bridge. Turn right to pass under bridge no 73.

From now on the towpath leading you back to Garstang takes you through tranquil pastures with dramatic views of the Bleasdale Fells away to the left. Look right to see Kiln Trees Farm, where bricks would have been made. Dawdle along the way where a myriad wild flowers thrive in summer, sheltered by the hedgerows. As you return to Garstang enjoy the herons that feed, the mallards that squabble, the moorhens that scurry over water and land alike, and the swans proudly shepherding their brood.

## WALK 22

*Knott End-on-Sea and Preesall*

| | |
|---|---|
| **Distance** | 9km (5½ miles) |
| **Time** | 3 hours |
| **Terrain** | Easy walking all the way |
| **Maps** | OS Explorer 296 |

Park in the car park, grid ref 346485, behind Knott End Café, once the terminus for the Pilling Pig, the old Garstang–Knott End railway. To reach the car park take

This is an invigorating walk. It takes you beside the wide, silvery estuary of the River Wyre and then continues through quiet hedged pastures. After winding round the edge of the village of Preesall the walk continues over more pastures to come to the grand footpath along the embankment above Preesall Sands. From here there are extensive views of Morecambe Bay and its teeming birdlife.

the last left turn off the B5270 before the road ends at the jetty. The café stands guardian over the point where the River Wyre surges out into Morecambe Bay.

Leave the car park by its entrance and wind round left in front of the café. Walk left again to stroll the narrow, walled promenade upstream of the river, the estuary to your right. Look across to the skyline of Fleetwood with its fine imposing buildings, and perhaps two or more large boats waiting to leave on the tide. If the tide is on the ebb you should see oystercatchers, redshank and shelduck probing the sandbanks and tidal gutters.

Just before Sea Dyke Cottage (dated 1754) and another dwelling, turn left away from the estuary path on a signposted track and wind

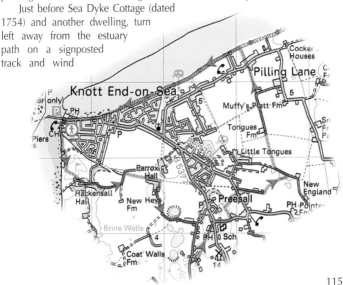

*Fleetwood across the Wyre estuary*

right behind the two houses to follow the footpath as it swings right. It then continues uphill close to the cliff edge and along the side of the golf course. Follow the path to a signpost and then, with care (golf balls), strike diagonally across the links towards woodland to join a farm track.

Walk right past a pond on the left, part-edged with willows, and then into woodland. Follow the waymark directing you left to walk along a lane beside a fence on your right. You might wish to walk a short way along the first right turn to see fine Jacobean Hackensall Hall. Return to the lane and carry on along the now tarmacked way to where it winds sharp left.

Here, go ahead on another pleasing track. Follow this route until you come to a gravelled right turn to walk the bed of the old Pilling railway. Pass through more pastures and then, at the end of a small wood on your right, go through an iron kissing gate on the right to climb a steepish slope to a waymarked stile into the farmyard of Curwens Hill. Continue ahead along the access track as it gently descends through more pastures. Continue past several fishing lakes on either side of the track, and go on where the way becomes metalled before reaching a T-junction at Preesall's Town Foot.

Turn right and walk the delightful narrow lane until you have passed a row of dwellings called Fern Beck Cottages. Turn left and then take the hedged footpath sharp left known as Lindal Lane. Go ahead along this most pleasing way until you reach the B5377 and cross with care. Walk directly ahead along the road to pass St Aidan's Technical College, and then descend until you spot a flight of steps climbing the slope on the opposite side of the road. Cross and ascend to a kissing gate. Beyond, strike diagonally left and gently uphill to the corner of Preesall's primary school. Then take a stile into a railed grassy track running along behind the playground. At the end of the fenced way leave the track by a stile on the right. Pause here to enjoy the splendid views of the Fylde Plain and the Forest of Bowland beyond.

Once over the stile descend the steepish slope to a footbridge over a ditch. Stride on along a clear path to climb a stile, then walk for 20 steps to take another stile onto a fenced footpath that leads to a stile onto a road. Cross, turn left, and then right into Gaulters Lane, a hedged track that leads into the flat pastures beyond Preesall. Look for the fascinating small windmill in the grounds of a modern house.

*Hackensall Hall, Knott End*

At the end of the lane, just before the gate ahead into pastures, turn left to walk a signposted narrow strip of grass between a ditch and the fence of a cottage. Climb a stile into a pasture and cross this on a right diagonal to a footbridge over another ditch. If this part of the walk is under water, go through the gate, wind left round the flooding, then bear right to climb the next stile. Go on in the same general direction between two fishing ponds, and then left again along a narrow strip of land between two more of the ponds. At the end of this strip go through a signposted (on the far side) stile onto a wide track where you walk left.

Where the track divides take the right branch to pass between flat, treeless arable land. Stride on, ignoring as you go the several footpaths that lead off left and right. Where the lane eventually swings sharp right, continue ahead along a narrow path between a deep ditch to the left and a large industrial building on the right. Once past the latter go on the stiled way, remaining beside the ditch. Carry on until you reach Pilling Lane and cross to climb a stone stepped stile.

Dawdle along the stiled path with the ditch to your right and climb steps up to the embankment. Turn left and walk the glorious breezy path where huge limestone boulders have been piled high as part of the sea defence. From the path look back to see Black Combe and the continuing line of the Lakeland hills, with Barrow's submarine shed rearing tall and white over the waters of the bay. The path continues for 2.4km (1½ miles) and returns you to Knott End and the esplanade. Head on to take the last left turn on the left to reach the car park behind the café.

# WALK 23

## *Skippool Creek, Wyre Estuary*

| | |
|---|---|
| **Distance** | 13km (8 miles) |
| **Time** | 3–4 hours |
| **Terrain** | Easy, level walking all the way; to avoid road walking return to Skippool by the same route |
| **Maps** | OS Explorer 296 |

The River Wyre rises in the Forest of Bowland, and after flowing through small villages and towns carries on – wide and sinuous – to enter the sea at Fleetwood. Beside or close by the river for much of its length runs a long-distance footpath called the Wyre Way, and several routes in this book direct walkers along charming stretches of it.

As the footpath nears the docks at Fleetwood it turns inland and continues along roads to cross the narrow penninsula and join the Lancashire Coastal Way at Rossall. The walk along the shore from Skippool to Stanah visitor centre is a delight. Beyond, the path eventually passes beside the ICI Hillhouse International chemical works, which uses brine pumped out of the deliberately flooded Preesall salt mines on the other side of the estuary. The water is then piped across the estuary to the works.

Park in the Wyre Estuary Country Park at Skippool, grid ref 356411. To reach this, take the B5412 at the round-about where the A588 and the A585 meet, and after 100 metres turn right into Wyre Road. The large car park and picnic area lies on the left at the end of the short metalled way.

Return to the Wyre Way, now a reinforced track, and walk left with the deep, picturesque Skippool Creek beside you on the right. Go on beside the River Wyre. Look right for a brief glimpse of Shard Bridge, a long elegant structure on stone pillars which carries the

*Path beside the Wyre at Skippool*

A588, the last crossing over the river before it empties into the sea. Walk on along the riverside by the Blackpool and Fylde Yachting Club clubhouse. If the tide is out you might see green plovers, gulls and redshanks out on the sandbanks.

You then pass the amazing sight of more than 100 slatted jetties stretching out over the turf, and then the estuarine mud, to stand on legs in the waters of the Wyre. Some jetties have rusting boats beside them; some boats are in use, others derelict. To the left the path is shadowed by beech and hawthorn, where blue, great and long-tailed tits can be seen. Beyond the moorings the track leads into the open countryside, with tidal gutters and salt marsh to the right and pastures to the left. Follow the riverside path as it winds past a small gutter, and then continues on the reinforced way around the large curve in the river. Walk on along the path with salt marsh to your right. Close to the water grow cord-grass, glasswort and marsh samphire, and nearer to land flourish sea aster, sea-purslane, sea-blite, sea lavender, sea arrowgrass and sea plantain. Continue to the site of a tiny, isolated 19th-century dwelling known as **Cockle Hall**.

## COCKLE HALL

Cockle Hall was named after a great cockle bed in the nearby river. Because it was so remote the original tenant, the father of 13 children, described himself as 'the only squire this side of the Wyre'. In 1989 the small site was developed and picnic tables added so that it could be enjoyed by those of limited mobility.

Once through the picnic area the path moves into a hedged way. Ignore the next two footpaths leading off left and walk on. Follow the good track to pass through the car park of the Wyre Estuary Country Park at Stanah. (There are toilets at the nearby visitor centre.) Carry on to walk round a very small creek and continue along a narrow waymarked path which passes between hedges. Climb the stile and continue on the hedged way. You then pass the ICI chemical works, a large building with chimneys and a great tangle of pipes. From here you can just glimpse where the Wyre discharges its waters into the sea, and perhaps a large boat leaving Fleetwood Docks. Stroll on beside ICI's tall fence on the left. Eventually most of the industrialisation and some dereliction are left behind, and you continue to walk on beside railings beyond which there is a large rectangular pond where coot may be seen.

Soon the Wyre Way winds sharp left and continues on a grassy trod with railings on both sides to come to a disused railway line. Cross the

121

*River Wyre with Bleasdale Fells in distance*

track and climb a stile. Beyond, walk the delightful 800-metre (½-mile) embanked path as it runs above the vegetation on either side, shadowed for all its length by pleasing hedges. This enjoyable way ends at the B5268.

At this point the walk returns by your outward route. As you go, enjoy the ever-changing views of, and from, the ever-changing river. Beyond you have dramatic views of Lancashire's sombre fells.

# WALK 24

## *Bleasdale Fells*

| | |
|---|---|
| **Distance** | 12km (7½ miles) |
| **Time** | 4 hours |
| **Terrain** | Pleasing, steepish grassy way onto Parlick and Fair Snape Fell; after a rainy spell do not venture over the peat hags of Holme House Fell; some of the farm tracks are muddy after rain if used by cattle |
| **Maps** | OS Explorer OL41 |

This is a great walk of contrasts. It starts with an exhilarating climb to the top of Parlick and then on up to Fair Snape Fell. After descending to Bleasdale the route takes you through lush pastures and deciduous woodland, with a brief detour to see Bleasdale Circle. This raised barrow is a Bronze Age burial mound, once enclosed by a circle of wooden posts, a palisade and a dyke. The remnants of the posts are to be found in a Preston museum, and they have been replaced by some rather inappropriate squat concrete pillars. The site was discovered in 1898.

Park in an unsignposted layby, grid ref 602443, indicated on the OS map as a car park. The layby is found at the beginning of the lane to Fell Foot, which leaves to the left at the point where Startifants Lane makes a sharp right turn. There are several more laybys further up this lane, but on a good day these will be used by paragliders so it is wise to get there early.

Walk up the metalled lane towards Fell Foot with the large bulk of Parlick beyond. Go through the gate beside

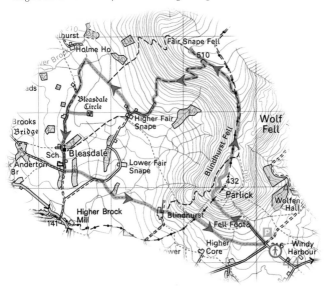

the house and climb the continuing pitched path. Bear left at the top and walk a distinct path that ascends steadily, enjoying as you go the superb views to Morecambe Bay across many miles of Lancashire.

Continue climbing to take a stile over a fence. Walk ahead for a few steps to the corner of a wall, and then turn right to begin zigzagging up the easy-to-walk turf with the fence away to your right. At the unmarked summit you reach another ladderstile over the fence and there are more spectacular views from here.

Descend the north side of Parlick. Ignore the 'open access' stile at the foot of the slope and continue on, gently climbing up lovely Blindhurst Fell. ◄ Soon the path moves away from the wall on your right and carries on up to climb a stile over another fence. Stroll on up through great cushions of bilberry and go on over a cross of paths (your return route) to ascend to a large cairn known as Paddy's Pole. Just beyond is a rough stone shelter with four sections, allowing you to get out of the wind from whichever direction it is blowing. Then walk on over the barren summit (510m (1683ft)) to the trig point from where there is another extensive view into Cumbria, Yorkshire and a vast part of Lancashire.

Return to the cross of paths and turn right to begin you descent from Fair Snape Fell on a wide, zigzagging permissive track. This was constructed and used by those with peat rights to bring down peat from the moor on sledges. Enjoy this grassy, well-graded way descending so easily through banks of bilberry. Climb a ladderstile and bear slightly right to continue zigzagging down the slope to a step stile over a wall. Beyond, go on down to climb another ladderstile, then follow a grassy sunken track. Continue where it swings right to the collection of dwellings at Higher Fair Snape.

Pass through the gated farmyard to wind on to a three-armed signpost. Here take a gated track (northwest) through pastures in the direction of Holme House. Stroll the continuing grassy path, with a ditch to the right, and keep ahead where it becomes indistinct. Cross the ditch on a tractor bridge and then go on along the other side

*Just before you reach a 'nick' or dip in the ridge look back to see an interesting rock formation, named Nick's Chair on the map.*

*An old peat track*

*Bleasdale Circle, a raised barrow, ditch and concrete post holes*

of the little stream. Walk on to the next signpost, just before a boundary wall, and turn left to stroll a permissive path. Go through a gate to join an access track and pass a signpost directing you on to Bleasdale Circle. Pass below several trees and then turn left, as directed by the signpost, for the permissive path to the circle. This takes you across a pasture to a kissing gate in the far left corner, and then on in the same direction to go through another gate into the mixed woodland that encloses the circle. After a pause in this magical corner walk on to a gap on the edge of the wood. Ahead lie Fair Snape Fell and Blindhurst Fell. Look for the dip in the ridge – perhaps at a certain time of year the rising sun shone over the dip onto the henge, or ring of wooden posts, in the circle.

Return along the permissive path to rejoin the track and turn left. Walk on to pass the Parish Church of St Eadmer of Admarsh in Bleasdale. Ignore the turn off to the right and continue on past the school. Just beyond, take a stile on the left, waymarked and with a 'Walkers welcome' sign. Walk ahead across a pasture and through a narrow belt of trees. Emerge from the woodland by a stile and go ahead over a pasture to a stile onto a narrow lane. Go left along the lane with, to your left, the fine semicircle of fells walked earlier.

Before the next cattle-grid turn right to walk a pleasing grassy trod. Cross the footbridge over the narrow River Brock and the step stile beyond. Carry on for a short distance beside a tributary stream to your left, and then follow the path as it moves away from the stream and to the next stile. Join a farm track that climbs up to Blindhurst farm. Go through the waymarked gate and cross the cobbled yard to wind left round the charming, white-painted farmhouse. Go through a gate and wind right, ignoring the path up onto the fells.

Waymarks on the fence to your right direct you along a rising grassy trod to pass through a hawthorn hedge with a waymark beyond. Ignore the stiles on your left giving 'open access' onto the fell, and go on to the top left corner of two fences where there is a stile. Beyond this cross a small stream. Wind right along a little path and then head across a large pasture towards a bright yellow disk on a tall pole. This marks a beautifully constructed step stile over the wall. Stride on, keeping well above a row of trees to your right, and take a stile in the next wall. Go on ahead, keeping to the same contour. There is another tiny stream to cross on stones, and then continue to a stile near the lower corner of the next boundary – ahead you can see Pendle Hill and Longridge Fell. Now make a beeline over the next pasture to the stile in the bottom right corner, and the parking area lies just beyond.

## WALK 25

### Hurst Green and Cromwell Bridge

| | |
|---|---|
| **Distance** | 11.4km (7 miles) |
| **Time** | 3–4 hours |
| **Terrain** | Easy walking all the way, mostly on good paths, tracks and lanes |
| **Maps** | OS Explorer 287 |

From the parking area at Hurst Green a short walk brings you to magnificent Stonyhurst College, a Roman Catholic boarding school. The towering gate-house at the end of the vista of lawn and ornamental canals is breathtaking. The building of the many-towered mansion was started by Sir Richard Shireburn in 1592. His descendants added numerous additions and lived there for a century or more. Neglect and a change of ownership followed, and in 1794 the house was offered to the Society of Jesus as temporary accommodation for their school – they are still there.

The walk takes you past fine Lower Hodder Bridge and then along a path to view Old Hodder Bridge, built in 1562 also by Richard Shireburn. It is generally called Cromwell Bridge and legend has it that Cromwell's troops crossed it at the time of the Battle of Preston.

JRR Tolkien spent some time at New Lodge, now a staff house for Stonyhurst College, while his son was studying for the priesthood there, and another son was classics master at the college. It was during the author's vis-its here that he started writing *The Fellowship of the Ring*. Were the fictional rivers Brandywine, Shirebourne and Withywindle inspired by the rivers Hodder, Ribble and Calder?

Originally alms-houses built at Kemple End in 1706 by Sir Nicholas Shireburn, they were removed piece by piece and reassem-bled at Hurst Green.

Park in the large gravelled area in front of Hurst Green parish hall, grid ref 684383, where you are asked to make a small donation for its upkeep. Turn right and pass some attractive estate workers cottages built in 1946. ◄ Carry on walking up the road, on the wide grassy verge, as it passes through fine woodland. Where the road turns right, pause to admire a tall statue of the Virgin Mary standing proud on a grassy mound. Then follow the road with the splendid mansion ahead reflected on the surface of the two large sheets of still water between which you pass.

Head on to the front of the college and turn right to walk beside the gracious chapel on the left. Follow the waymark directing you ahead beside the high wall of the tennis courts, next on your left. Wind left with the wall and continue on to reach Hall Barn Farm. At the two waymarked tracks take the left turn. Go on ahead along the traffic-free way, with Pendle Hill to the right, to reach another lane.

*Stonyhurst College*

Cross the lane and take a step to the left to walk a signposted metalled way and then a reinforced track. Where the track winds left follow the signposted path, continuing over a pasture to walk along the side of woodland on your left. Near the corner of the pasture take a stile into woodland and walk on along a delightful path through the trees. To your left, steep tree-clad slopes drop down to a tributary of the River Hodder.

*Cromwell Bridge, the popular name for Lower Hodder Bridge*

Descend the stepped way through the woodland to cross a footbridge over the stream and go on through the trees. Once you have passed a small, newly restored bridge over a tributary stream, turn right and climb the track through the trees to come to Hodder Place on your right. Here continue beside the very high wall of the dwelling on your right and descend steadily to go through a kissing gate. Continue ahead on a track with forest trees sloping down to the Hodder on your left, and delectable fields stretching away to your right.

Stroll on to the next kissing gate, which gives access to the fine Lower Hodder Bridge. Cross the B6246 with care, go through a narrow gap with the river still to your left, and walk the short path to come to Old Hodder Bridge, also known as Cromwell Bridge. There is no access to the bridge, but you may want to use your camera from close to the barbed wire guarding this lovely ancient monument. Here you must return to the road bridge because there is no continuing right of way.

Turn left (west) to walk the Ribble Way using the pavement along the fairly busy road. Continue uphill for 300 metres to a junction of roads where you take a signposted ladderstile on the left. Walk ahead across a field to take the next stile. Go on ahead uphill to go through another stile. Keep beside the wood on your left until you near a fence bisecting the pasture to your right. Then head right to take the waymarked kissing gate halfway along the fence. Beyond, head on in the same direction to take a kissing gate onto a road just beyond a small ruined building.

Walk left past Winckley Hall and carry on where the road becomes a track. Remain on the way to pass the outbuildings of Winckley Hall Farm and the duck pond, which once powered a water wheel. Still on the track, bear left through more buildings and then turn right to continue along a rough track, a wall to the right and a hedge to the left, and go through a gate. Here, hidden in summer by the dense vegetation, the waters of the Hodder unite with the River Ribble.

Stride on along the grassy path beside the delectable Ribble and continue to follow it as it makes a wide, gracious curve. Here the River Calder adds its waters to the Ribble. On the far bank, beyond the Calder, stands magnificent Hacking Hall, a Jacobean house with many mullioned windows. Follow the path past a new house set well back from the riverbank. ▶

Carry on beside the river and then follow a continuing path with a hedge to the right. This leads on above the Ribble and joins a metalled road. In a short distance the road turns inland and you go ahead on a waymarked grassy trod above the river. Stroll on along the pleasing stiled way to reach an aqueduct across the water, which you pass by climbing another stile. Continue on for a short way to the edge of deciduous woodland. Here look for a waymarked stile giving access to a footbridge over a little stream. Climb steps up through the trees to a stile into a pasture.

Go ahead with more woodland to the right. Follow the path as it moves into the trees and down steps to cross another footbridge. Climb a little through the trees to take a boardwalk to a stile. Carry on along a good path, keeping a ditch to your right. At the waymark cross an earth bridge over a ditch and head up to the top left corner of the pasture. Here, climb a step stile over a wall to the left of a gate and walk through the car park of the Shireburn Arms at Hurst Green. Cross the road and walk up the road ahead to the car park.

This was the site of the Boat House, once used to house the ferryman who took travellers across the Ribble between Winckley and Hacking.

# WALK 26

## Whalley

| | |
|---|---|
| **Distance** | 9km (5½ miles) |
| **Time** | 3 hours |
| **Terrain** | Easy walking for most of the route; steep climb out of Whalley; some paths can be muddy after rain; very little road walking but some very busy roads to cross |
| **Maps** | OS Explorer 287 |

The picturesque ruins of Whalley Abbey stand among trees in a glorious sheltered valley. The abbey belonged to the Cistercian order, and although no picture exists of the original structure, finished in the 1440s, the ruins and records give the impression of a magnificent building. Close by is the ancient Church of St Mary. Pause in the churchyard to view the Celtic crosses, possibly dating from the 10th century, and the many old gravestones. The construction of the present church began in about 1200 and it is worth allowing yourself plenty of time to enjoy the lovely building (generally open in the afternoons). Look for the Catterall Brass and marvel at the couple's 20 children, and visit the exquisitely carved choir stalls, originally made for the abbey and installed in the church after the dissolution of the monasteries in the 1530s. Spring Wood is a semi-natural ancient woodland. It was once owned by the monks of the abbey and was part of a deer park before being seized by the Crown at the time of the dissolution.

This walk takes you through lovely Lancashire countryside and along the banks of the stately River Calder.

Park at Spring Wood picnic site, grid ref 741361. This lies on the east side of the A671, the Whalley–Easterly bypass, less than 800 metres (½ mile) from the village itself. Here there are toilets and an unstaffed information centre.

Take the limited-mobility track going left out of the top left corner of the picnic site and follow it to a

Y-junction. Here go left through a kissing gate and pass under the A671. Continue over a muddy patch to a wall gap and a stile and then carry on along the continuing path, passing through pleasing bluebell woodland. Emerge from the trees and turn right to descend beside the hedge to a stile in the bottom right corner of the field. Beyond, join a track

*Gatehouse to Whalley Abbey*

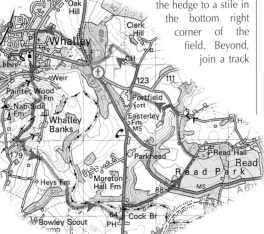

and bear left towards the village of Whalley. Go through the gate to a road and turn left at the three-armed sign-post, to then wind right and join King Street, where you turn left. Saunter on to take the pedestrian crossing and after a few steps turn right in front of the De Lacy Arms. Go past the church on your left (leaving your visit for later) and then the school to turn left and pass below the huge, turreted gatehouse of Whalley Abbey (entrance fee). Wander through the lovely grounds and roofless cloisters and perhaps sit awhile to enjoy the tranquillity.

Return beneath the gatehouse to the road and turn right. As you go through the Square look left to see some ancient buildings once used to store fishing equipment for the abbey, and then visit the very fine Parish Church of St Mary.

After leaving the church continue to King Street and turn right. Walk past the shops and cross Whalley Bridge, high above the River Calder. Cross the road with care and begin the steepish climb up Moor Lane, which goes off half left at the end of the bridge. After 100 metres, where the road swings right bear left to climb a reinforced path below magnificent beech trees. At a strategically placed seat for enjoying the wonderful view over the village, take the rough, walled bridlepath on the right to continue climbing.

When you reach the edge of a beech wood take the waymarked turn right and go on beside the wood, now on your left. Carry on to cross a concrete access track by stiles and continue climbing beneath more beeches. Walk on, keeping beside the fence to your left and following it as it swings left to a wall. Go on right and look for the waymark on a tree trunk directing you left to an easy-to-miss stile in the corner of the garden of a house. Then climb the stile immediately on your left, out of the garden, and walk right along the garden boundary to another stile back into the garden.

Stride the access track that runs ahead, with the house now to your right. Follow the way either through a gate or over a stile and then go on along the good track to join a lane. Descend left to pass a house, Woodhaven, and take the unsignposted (at the time of writing) foot-path on the right. The gate to the footpath looks like a piece of the fence on either side of it and the catch is on the far side of the gate. The gate leads along the left boundary wall of the garden of the house to a footbridge and then a stile. Beyond is a very wet patch. Climb the next stile and carry on, keeping to the left branch of the way through dense conifers where the trees are marked with yellow paint to direct you. Follow the path, now delineated by yellow-topped posts, as it drops downhill to a stile into a pasture.

Continue downhill, drifting slightly right, to a stile to a farm track which you cross to another stile to the left of a barn. Keep downhill to a stile in the bottom right corner of a pasture. Beyond, continue ahead keeping to the right side of a small stream to reach a stile. Once over, step across the stream and continue beside it soon to cross again on a fine clapper bridge. Stride ahead, following the path and take the left branch at a Y-junction to give you a first glimpse of the white-topped River Calder. Continue on to pass through a straggly hedge and then bear left towards the Calder where, beyond the fence, a narrow path runs beside the river to another clapper bridge over Dean Brook. Go on to take the ladderstile into Dean Wood and turn right to climb the stepped path beneath beeches.

Stroll on along the lovely high-level path through the woodland, with glorious views to the Calder below, to come to a large stone seat and a kissing gate. Beyond the gate turn left and descend the steep path through elegant parkland with the hurrying river to your left. Carry on beside the Calder and use boulders to cross Egg Syke Brook before walking on to cross Rodger Hey Brook by a footbridge. Beyond the next stile strike out towards some cottage rooftops that you can just spot ahead and to the right. The stile in the wall to the left of the cottages gives access to the A680. Cross with care and turn left to walk across Cock Bridge over the River Calder.

Turn right beyond the bridge to walk the lane until you reach a garden centre. Here take the signposted

*Martholme Viaduct*

track, to the left of the entrance, that runs beside Cock Wood. Stride the wide track and as you go look right to see the elegant stone Martholme Viaduct. Continue to Whalley Road, A671, crossing again with care, and pass through the splendid gates of Read Park at the beginning of the track into the parkland. At a Y-junction take the left fork, and turn left after a very short distance to climb a stile and go on along a grassy track with Coppy Plantation, a woodland overgrown with rhododendrons, to your right. Follow the track as it continues to a stile. Beyond, stroll on to a gate to join the old Roman road.

Here go left to cross Read Old Bridge over Sabden Brook and then walk uphill to take an access track sign-posted Easterley Farm. Climb the stile in the hedge on the right, just beyond the first gate. Beyond, strike slightly left uphill to a stile over the fence. Go straight ahead to take the next one, and beyond this strike half right to another stile in the boundary hedge. Climb the slope ahead, again bearing slightly right, to the right of the dwellings at Portfield and to a stile onto a lane.

Turn right and then right again onto a B road also named Whalley Road on the map. Cross over and after

20 metres, where the road swings right, walk ahead along a lane signposted 'Cul-de-sac'. Continue ahead until just past the access track to the clubhouse of Whalley golf course. Here take the stone step stile in the wall on the left and walk across the large pasture to climb a further stile. Stroll on to a fence with a yellow band on one of its posts. Beyond, turn and walk down the slope to cross a footbridge over a stream and on to the golf course. Here walkers are reminded to watch out for golf balls.

Continue round the right edge of the golf course, and as you near the A671 look for the concessionary path that winds right to a stile into the car park.

## WALK 27

### *Downham*

| Distance | 9.5km (6 miles) |
|----------|-----------------|
| Time | 4 hours |
| Terrain | Generally easy walking with very few steep slopes to climb; well waymarked |
| Maps | OS Explorer OL41 |

Downham, the village often described as east Lancashire's prettiest, sits on the slope of a limestone hill close to a Roman road that linked York with Ribchester. Downham Hall, built in the 16th century, is the home of the Assheton family (Lord Clitheroe) and through the centuries they have preserved the village, allowing nothing to mar its picturesque charm. For example there are no pylons to spoil the beauty of the village – the cables have all been laid below ground.

This route takes you below several delightful hills, reef-knolls deposited millions of years ago when the area was below the sea.

The walk starts from Downham's unobtrusive free car park, grid ref 785441, which has excellent facilities and

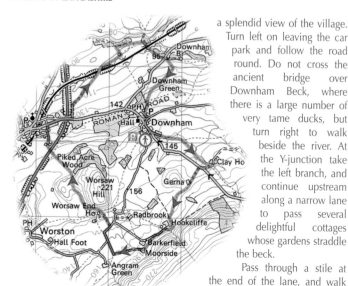

a splendid view of the village. Turn left on leaving the car park and follow the road round. Do not cross the ancient bridge over Downham Beck, where there is a large number of very tame ducks, but turn right to walk beside the river. At the Y-junction take the left branch, and continue upstream along a narrow lane to pass several delightful cottages whose gardens straddle the beck.

Pass through a stile at the end of the lane, and walk the arrowed way over a meadow to climb a stile in the far right corner. Continue beside a tributary stream, now to your left, along the field edge. Cross a footbridge and carry on with a fence to your right and woodland to your left. As you near Clay House farm take the wall stile on your right to join the access track to the farm. Turn right and walk to Pendle Road.

Cross and turn right. Almost immediately take the signposted footpath on the left to stroll the track to Gerna farm, tucked below the steep lower slopes of the whale-back of Pendle Hill. To the right stands Gerna Hill, the first of the reef-knolls seen on this walk. Where the track swings right to the dwelling, go ahead to take a step stile beside a metal gate and walk on to cross another stile. Go on through a gate and walk ahead towards the boundary wall and fence of Hookcliffe farm (dated 1714). Bear left, remaining in the large pasture, to climb up to a three-armed signpost and a stile on to a track that runs along the lower slopes of Pendle Hill.

Turn right and walk on to pass through a gate. After about 300 metres watch out for a gate on the left giving access to a continuing wide grassy shelf-like track. This leads to a ford and footbridge over a tumbling stream and to a gate. Pass through the outbuildings of Moorside farm and through a second gate to stride the long track to metalled West Lane, where you turn right. Ahead lies Worsaw Hill, another fine limestone reef-knoll.

Press on along the lane, and where it swings sharply left go on ahead, soon to wind right. A short distance along turn left into the waymarked left turn, the access track to Worsaw End House. Follow the track as it winds left and then step across the grass on the right to go through a gate. Beyond, join a good grassy track rising left and continue along below Worsaw Hill. Above, the slopes are covered with scattered hawthorn and gorse, and in many places the underlying limestone is exposed.

Look back for an extensive view of Pendle Hill and then saunter on level with the wall on your left, beyond which you can see the reef-knolls of Warren Hill, the Ridge and Crow Hill. Look at the stones of the wall to see the fossilised remains of thousands of tiny branchipods

*Pendle Hill seen from Downham walk*

139

and crinoids. Follow the path as it drifts away from the wall to pass between small hillocks and reach the top of the slope. Here a magnificent view of rural, rolling Lancashire awaits.

Descend the slope to climb a stile, and then go down a much steeper slope through scattered holly, blackthorn and hawthorn. Beyond, stride across a flat pasture to a stile in the far right corner of the wall. Stroll ahead over a large pasture towards some tall trees, crossing the faint course of the Roman road. A kissing gate to the left of a planting of young trees gives access to a slope up to the A59. Cross with great care, drop down the public footpath on the other side to a stile, and then follow the path right and then right again along a fenced grassy way into woodland. Carry on along the path to go over a stone stile.

Cross a muddy track and take a second stile opposite into the well-kept communal garden of several houses. Continue ahead over a wide grassy sward, keeping beside the hedge on your left, and then descend to cross the beck by a flat concrete bridge. Climb the easy-to-miss signposted steps to a gate on the outskirts of Chatburn. Beyond the gate, walk past the Methodist church on your left and then an attractive white house, Cayley Cottage (dated 1907), on your right. Continue along a ginnel and turn right onto Chatburn Road, lined with houses on either side.

Next, cross the high-level bridge over the A59 from where you have more spectacular views. At the end of the bridge cross Chatburn Road and take the stile to the left of a gate. Walk ahead along a track until you near the boundary, where you bear right along the side of a young hedge to pass through a kissing gate onto a good track. Carry on through two gates to cross a bridge over the railway line. Wind right along a grassy path that soon becomes hedged on both sides with hawthorn. Leave the 'tunnel of trees' to walk on through an open pasture with a hedge to your right. Go through the gate ahead and then a gate on your right. Walk on to pass in front of a stone barn and turn left to go through a gate.

Go across the middle of a pasture to reach the steep wooded slopes overlooking hurrying Smithies Brook. Do not descend the slope, but turn right and continue beside the fenced woodland on your left and high above the beck. Pass through a sturdy stile and descend the slope to cross a footbridge. Beyond, walk diagonally left to a wall and continue beside it until you come to a step stile over it. Then bear half left to come to Fairy Bridge, a fairytale packhorse bridge over the brook. It has no parapets to get in the way of the pack ponies' panniers.

*Fairy Bridge – an ancient packhorse bridge*

Return from the bridge to climb the step stile once more and go ahead to walk beside a mainly conifer wood, now on your left. Then go under a muddy railway bridge. Beyond, walk up the slope and look left through trees to see a splendid stone viaduct. Walk on beside a larch plantation to a stile onto Rimington Lane and cross over. Walk a few steps down the track opposite to take the signposted stile on the right.

Climb the slope, keeping to the right of the reef-knoll topped with lofty beeches. Just before the brow, bear right and head for the top of the steepish ridge and the trees at the far end. Pause here for an astounding view ahead and behind you. Keeping the wall of the wood on your right, drop down to a step stile and walk on to take the gate on the right into Downham. Walk ahead to visit the largely medieval Church of St Leonard, with its thick tower and gargoyles. Opposite the church is the Assheton Arms.

Continue down through the village, passing the stocks on your left and then the charming Steward's House, now two cottages. Cross the bridge and turn right to rejoin your car after a walk that seems to have something interesting or exciting to view round every corner.

# WALK 28

## *Weets Hill, Barnoldswick*

| | |
|---|---|
| **Distance** | 12km (7½ miles) |
| **Time** | 4 hours |
| **Terrain** | Steepish climb onto Weets Hill, and then nearly all down with a fine, level return along the towpath |
| **Maps** | OS Explorer OL 41 |

Start this walk from Barnoldswick, which used to be in Yorkshire but since the boundary changes of 1974 is now part of Lancashire. This pleasant small town shelters in a fine valley with slopes and hills all around. Nearest is Weets Hill (397m (1302ft)), from where there is a superb panoramic view. The return is made along a section of the Leeds–Liverpool Canal. This was constructed to provide a trans-Pennine waterway linking the emergent industrial towns of Yorkshire and Lancashire with the North American market via Liverpool. Work began at the same time from both ends, in Leeds and Liverpool, after the first Canal Act was passed in 1770.

Park in the long-stay car park opposite Barnoldswick police station, grid ref 877465. This lies above and to the west of the short-stay car park (2½ hours only) in the centre of the town.

Turn left out of the car park and descend right at the traffic lights a few steps along. At the next set of traffic lights turn left into Church Street to pass in front of the tourist information office. Walk on, soon to descend between the Cross Keys on the left and the Seven Stars on the right. Just beyond the pubs bear right onto Walmsgate and carry on steadily climbing. At Town Head follow the road as it winds left, and from where you can see Bancroft Mill chimney ahead. Then take the second turning on the right to walk along Moorgate Road.

Then begin to climb up the continuing hedged Folly Lane, which eventually becomes a reinforced track with pastures on either side. Just before a farm leave the track by a stile on the right signposted with a Pendle Way

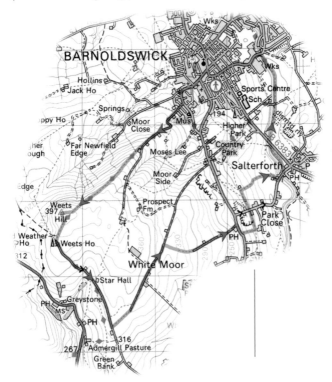

*Look back down on Barnoldswick to count the number of chimneys you can see. The town once had 17 cotton mills.*

waymark (a witch on a broomstick). Go on up quite steeply on a distinct path at the side of the pasture with a wall to your left. Climb a stile and carry on where the terrain begins to change from pasture to moorland. You will be tempted to pause often to enjoy the view. ◀

Continue on the stiled way, and when you have climbed the last one before the top you can look down a long ravine to the right. Carry on beside the wall to a Y-junction. Here take a grassy trod right, heading for a cairn on the brow. Beyond, a path continues over the plateau to the trig point on the summit of Weets Hill. From here you can see Pendle Hill and the Bowland Fells to the west and Penyghent and Ingleborough to the north. Just north of the trig point is a wooden seat – just right for your first break.

From the trig point take another grassy path that returns you to the side of the wall, and carry on downhill for a short distance to go through a large signposted gate in the wall. Walk to the left of Weets House to join the narrow, gravelled, traffic-free road, part of the Pendle Way and named Gisburn Old Road. From here you have a good view of Stansfield Tower on Blacko Hill. Carry on for about 1.6km (1 mile) until you are a short distance

*Barnoldswick seen from the way up Weets Hill*

144

before a white house (Peel's House). Here look for a bridleway on the left to pass through one of three gates.

Enjoy the walled grassy track, Lister Well Road, from where, over White Moor, you can spot reservoirs constructed in the 18th century as feeders for the canal. Carry on past a small copse of conifers, and stride on to a signposted gate on the right giving access to a grassy track through heather. Where it swings right to a pond, go ahead to a gate in the wall ahead. Then carry on to a fine step stile in the bottom left corner giving onto a long straight track. Descend this delightful walled way to pass Copy Nook farm and then on to join High Lane. Turn right to pass the Fanny Grey pub. Cross the lane with care and continue on for a short distance to descend the road-side banking to a stile.

Beyond, descend the slope towards Booth House Farm, and at the boundary wall turn left through the farm gate and walk ahead along the field edge to climb a stile in the corner. Ascend the slope onto the lawn of a house and follow the waymark directing you to the left of the dwelling. Where the lawn ends, turn right to climb stone steps to a lane and wind left to walk past more cottages to Salterford Road.

Turn left and almost immediately take the signposted footpath on the right. Walk through woodland which now clothes a disused quarry. Climb the rough, stepped way and then the stile out of the trees and walk on. Take an easy-to-miss stile on the right 100 metres beyond the start of a wall on your right. Drop downhill with a wall to your left and then descend to a gap stile to the left of a small stone building. Walk ahead to a stile giving access to a track, and pass a house on your right. Join its access track, which leads to the road. Turn left and cross Salterforth Bridge to the Anchor Inn. The inn was there before the canal was cut, and because the door was blocked off by the new embankment you now drink in what were once bedrooms, the ground floor having become the cellar.

Pass under the canal bridge and walk the towpath with the cut to your left. Very shortly pass through a small

*Walking the towpath of the Leeds–Liverpool Canal*

car park, and carry on along the path to pass Salterford moorings and then go under a road bridge. Carry on for 1.2km (¾ mile), passing Lower Park Marina and then the Silentnight factory, both on the opposite bank and on the edge of Barnoldswick. At the next bridge, a white metal one, leave the towpath, join the road and turn left to cross the bridge. Walk on, remaining on the fairly busy road until you arrive at the car park on your left, just before the traffic lights and the police station opposite.

## WALK 29

### Wycoller and Boulsworth Hill

| | |
|---|---|
| **Distance** | 12km (7½) miles |
| **Time** | 4 hours |
| **Terrain** | Good tracks and paths for most of the route; the climb over the peat of Boulsworth Hill can be wet underfoot; the route is well waymarked, but do not climb the hill in the mist |
| **Maps** | OS Explorer OL21 |

Wic-air is the Anglo-Saxon name for Wycoller and means the dairy farm among the alders. At one time this was the predominant tree in the area, then the land was cleared and the trees cut down. Today a young plantation of alders is thriving on the slopes above the little settlement. Enjoy this pleasing corner with its 13th-century twin-arched packhorse bridge and, further upstream, its clapper bridge. The clapper bridge is formed of two slabs supported by stone piers, and these slabs are worn to a trough-shape by the clogs of generations of weavers taking their cloth to the tenterfield (drying ground) above Wycoller Hall. Look up at the slope above the hall to see 13th-century vaccary walls, slabs of stone used as boundaries to enclose cattle. It is difficult to believe that 350 people lived in the settlement in 1820, but the villagers were handloom weavers and with the development of the powerloom they had to move away to find jobs.

The Bronte sisters visited Wycoller and the hall may have been the original for Ferndean Manor in *Jane Eyre*. By 1950 the hamlet was almost deserted.

Park in the car park at the end of Trawden Road, grid ref 926396, above the village of Wycoller. Leave by the footpath which runs downhill from the southeast end and joins the narrow lane into the hamlet. Wind right to pass the teashop and art gallery to come to the tiny two-arched packhorse bridge across the beck. Walk on to the clapper bridge, which you might like to cross to explore the ruin of fine Wycoller Hall, with its magnificent fireplace.

Return across the clapper bridge, taking the sign-posted tarmacked lane opposite to ascend steadily away from the beck. After a short climb look for the waymarked path on the right. Climb the stepped way through lush vegetation to a gate and continue through deciduous woodland. Ignore the right turn, and go on up to the end of the trees to climb a three-way stile with Raven's Rock Farm away to the left. Pause to take in the magnificent view of east Lancashire with Pendle Hill towering over all.

Stride on along the stiled way to wind right round the outside of the wall of Germany Farm. Climb the stile in

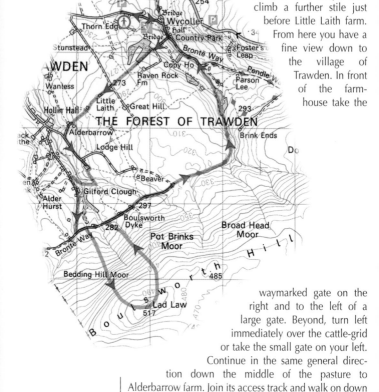

the corner and carry on to climb a further stile just before Little Laith farm. From here you have a fine view down to the village of Trawden. In front of the farm-house take the

waymarked gate on the right and to the left of a large gate. Beyond, turn left immediately over the cattle-grid or take the small gate on your left. Continue in the same general direction down the middle of the pasture to Alderbarrow farm. Join its access track and walk on down to a narrow lane where you turn left.

Continue to where the lane swings sharp left and walk ahead along a signposted track. Keep to the left of farm buildings and go on along the good gated track as it winds right and descends the slope to cross a tractor bridge over a hurrying beck. Turn right and walk the delightful grassy sward as it rises above a pretty beck. Look on the far side for a waterfall, tumbling down rocks in haste to join the main beck. Then go on to pause on the high ground to see, across the beck, the splendid single white fall of water that is Lumb Spout, descending elegantly into a dark brown pool at the foot of a verdant hollow.

Stroll on over a stile and, still with the beck to your right, wind on round and past some pleasing cascades to reach a sturdy footbridge at a junction of streams. Beyond, wind right to cross a much longer footbridge and follow the well-signed public footpath. Climb the next stile and go on, ignoring the footbridge on the right. Follow the path as it climbs a slope, bear sharp left at the waymark, then strike up right over the rough grass to a gap stile onto a track. Here you turn left.

At Tongue End Farm, where there is a gate across the track, take the small signposted gate to a path on the left. Follow the way and continue as it swings right and carries on to a stile into Gilford Clough, where a stream chuckles away to your left. Cross the ford or the footbridge and walk on to a rising boardwalk to join a good track.

Turn left, and a few steps along look for the signpost directing you up the well-waymarked permissive path which takes a circular route over the moorland slopes of Boulsworth Hill. ▶ At first the path climbs gently and

If when you reach this part of the walk the weather has deteriorated, ignore the hill walk and continue on the track to reach the metalled way at the water-treatment plant.

*Lad Low, Boulsworth Hill*

there are several tiny peaty ditches to cross. Beyond the stile over the fence the path becomes steeper and drier and leads to the dramatic Abbot Stone. From here there is a fine view of Lower and Upper Coldwell reservoirs. Press on over the now flatter, wetter moorland plateau, where you will have to pick your way more carefully to arrive at the trig point on Lad Law (517m (1706ft)). There are extensive views from here.

Carry on along the waymarked path, winding round the peaty parts, to come to the magnificent Weather Stones. The path takes you through these intriguing boulders and then descends quite steeply to another clump of boulders, Little Chair Stones. From now on the waymarked route becomes much drier and easier to walk and descends to a kissing gate through a fence. The path then heads on down easily to join a concrete way beside a small, covered water-treatment plant.

Follow the concrete way to join the track you were on before your ascent of the hill. Turn right along the now metalled way and continue to the end of the tarmac. Ignore the turns left and right and go ahead through a kissing gate to climb a short rough slope. Then carry on by the wall on your left, often treading the remaining stones of an ancient paved way. To your right is the very deep Saucer Hill Clough and, beyond, steep lonely moorland stretching away southeast.

Follow the distinct path as it winds slightly left, keeping to the wall with the deep clough beside you. Continue on down, and when you can spot lonely Brink Ends farmhouse high above to your right you will arrive at a signpost with many waymarks on it. Here you go ahead on the Brontes in Pendle circular walk to climb a stile to the left of a gate.

Almost immediately descend the concessionary path, dropping right to walk above Turnhole Clough. At the bottom of the slope climb a stile into a glorious hollow beside the bubbling stream, and then ascend the slope to a waymark with the beck carrying on through the mixed deciduous woodland. Walk on beside the fenced woodland on your right to come to a kissing gate into the

The 'clam' bridge at Wycoller

trees and follow the path as it descends to the beck on the right. Do NOT cross the footbridge, but go through the gate on your left and follow the path beside the fence on your right until you reach the next footbridge, which you do cross.

Wind on round beside the beck, now to your left, until you can pass through a kissing gate onto a lane where you continue left. A few metres along, spanning the beck, stands the 'clam' bridge, a single slab of gritstone. ▶

Carry on to Wycoller. Here you may wish to while away some time before climbing the lane and then the footpath to rejoin your car.

The bridge probably dates from the Iron Age. It appears precariously balanced on the lane side but is in fact quite firm and safe.

# WALK 30

## *Pendle Hill*

| | |
|---|---|
| **Distance** | 10km (6 miles) |
| **Time** | 3–4 hours |
| **Terrain** | Steepish pitched climb onto Pendle Hill; flagged paths across moorland; narrow stony paths through Ogden Clough; two streams to cross – might be troublesome after heavy rain |
| **Maps** | OS Explorer OL41 |

Pendle Hill (557m (1831ft)) dominates the landscape for miles around. Its great whaleback shape broods over the attractive villages of Barley, Downham, Roughlee, Twiston and Newchurch, all set in glorious Lancashire countryside. Closely associated with the hill are the Pendle witches: 10, all of whom lived on farms and in villages about the hill, were sent to the scaffold at Lancaster and at York in 1612. But not all the associations with the hill are fearsome – it was Pendle Hill that inspired George Fox to found the Quaker movement.

Enjoy the many kissing gates on this walk that have been constructed to provide easy access for walkers and their rucksacks. The path to the top of Pendle Hill has been stepped in local stone and blends well with the slopes. The stepped way across the peat hags is a wonderful piece of work – you could dance across the moor admiring the flags and not notice the depth of some of the boggy holes on either side.

Park in the attractive picnic site, grid ref 823404, close by the stream at Barley, northwest of Barrowford. Leave the parking area by a footpath that starts beyond the toilet block. Cross a pleasing grassed area across the road from the Pendle Inn, then stride a footbridge over the stream and go on along the footpath to come to the Barley Mow pub. Carry on past a tearoom and then cross the road to take the signposted track, the Pendle Way, in the direction of Pendle Hill.

Go through a kissing gate and on to cross a footbridge. Carry on over a large pasture to descend a bank on the right. Cross a stream and go on along a tarmacked track. Keep to the right where the way soon divides, ignoring the grassy footpath left, and take the metalled way towards a group of dwellings. Bear to the left of the first house, following 'path' signs painted on the access

*The way up*
*Pendle Hill*

track. A short way along turn right through a metal kissing gate onto a cobbled way, as directed by a large sign that says 'This way to Pendle Hill'.

Walk ahead to cross a footbridge and go on through a gap stile into pastures where there are alders about the stream and the hill towering over you. Keep on through a kissing gate and onto a track. Pass a cottage on the left and go on through the next gate to bear right along a farm track. In a few steps take another gate on the left and press on through two more kissing gates. Then go through another to the left of Pendle House. Beyond, bear right to a kissing gate in the top right corner to come to the start of the ladder-like stepped way to the top of the hill. As you climb look right to see the two Black Moss reservoirs, the upper completed in 1894 and the lower in 1903.

The easy path leads up and up. Regular pauses are recommended to catch your breath and to savour the magnificent views that become ever more extensive. At the top of the steps a short path leads you to a stile in the boundary wall. Ignore this and turn left before the wall to follow a worn track across the large flat summit to the trig point. After another pause to enjoy the stunning view, continue on to a clear waymarker post for the Pendle

Hill circular walk. A few steps beyond and you stand at the start of the long flagged path that gently descends across the awesome heather moorland of Pendle Hill.

The end of the long track brings you to the stream in Ogden Clough, which you step across on stones to join a path going off left. Follow the easy way as it rises steadily above the stream and carries on along the side of the steep slopes into the depths of the lonely treeless hills. When you reach a waymark take the left branch to carry on along a narrow, very high concessionary path as it winds south through the continuing Ogden Clough. Watch out for the place where the path suddenly descends by easy zigzags to the side of the stream.

Step across on rough stones to join the path running through the clough on the opposite bank. Pass through a kissing gate and press on parallel with the stream, steep slopes towering on either side. Just beyond a Pendle Way sign cross a substantial stream, again on stones, and go on to descend a very rough track to a kissing gate. When Upper Ogden Reservoir is fully in view the wild lonely slopes have been left behind.

*Upper Ogden Reservoir*

155

The path carries on high above the reservoir at first and then descends to go through a gate. Go on along a delightful grassy way to pass the large dam. Ignore the path over the dam and descend steeply to a step stile beside a gate. Stride on along the access track, deciduous trees to the right and Scots pine to the left.

Remain on the wide track to pass through a kissing gate to go on beside Lower Ogden Reservoir. Beyond the dam descend a narrow lane below beeches. Pass the waterworks building on the left. This is built on the site of a cotton mill, one of five that thrived in the valley, but which was washed away in a great storm in 1880. After this the flood waters of the wayward river were harnessed by building the Ogden reservoirs. Go on to join the road at Barley. Cross and then go over the road bridge to return to the car park on the left.

# WALK 31

## Chipping and Dinkling Green

| | |
|---|---|
| **Distance** | 13km (8 miles) |
| **Time** | 4–5 hours |
| **Terrain** | Easy walking all the way; can be muddy about Leagram Brook and around the ford below High Greystoneley |
| **Maps** | OS Explorer OL41 |

Park in the car park, grid ref 623434, just west of Chipping's St Bartholomew's Church (there are toilets here). From the parking area join a road called Church Raikes which runs close to the side wall of the church. Walk left and at the Y-junction take the right fork to descend a narrow lane into a tiny settlement around Berry's chair factory. This is housed in an old cotton mill, built in 1840, and there are huge tree trunks to be seen, waiting to be cut on a great saw. Notice the neat

The picturesque village of Chipping lies on slopes above the River Loud. It is a conservation area with stone-built cottages, and a 17th-century school and almshouses endowed by John Brabin, a London dyer and cloth merchant. The church was first built in the 13th century and has been partly rebuilt several times since. The font has been in use for more than 400 years. One sad story linked with the church is that of Lizzy Dean, a 20-year-old 'serving wench' at the Sun Inn. She was engaged to be married to a local man, but, one morning in 1835, on hearing the church bells she looked out of the window of her room at the inn and saw her bridegroom leaving the church with another bride on his arm. She hanged herself in the attic of the pub. Her last request was that her grave be dug in the path to the church so that her ex-boyfriend had to walk over it every Sunday. This request was refused, and she is said still to haunt the Sun Inn.

The hamlet of Dinkling Green lies in a leafy hollow surrounded by limestone knolls and seems at least a couple of centuries behind most of the rest of Lancashire. Peace pervades, no motorway or railway impinging on the quietness of this lovely corner of the Forest of Bowland.

row of cottages with pretty gardens that were once the workhouse.

Continue uphill and look over the wall on the left to see the attractive millpond, a tranquil stretch of water almost surrounded by trees. Halfway along the side of the pond take the easy-to-miss signposted stile on the other side of the road. Climb straight up the grassy slope, with an ever-increasing view of the Bleasdale Fells, to a stile in the right-hand corner of the pasture. Continue ahead to the next stile, which stands under two trees between the right end of a fence and the left end of a very long wall. Beyond, walk on over rough ground to cross a small stream and continue parallel with the fence on your right to come to a stile in the top right corner, giving onto the access track to Birchen Lee (built in 1867).

Turn right and walk a wide track to a three-armed signpost. Go on in the same direction towards Chipping Lawn farm. Just before the first farm building leave the track left, as directed by waymarks, and head across the large pasture, keeping just to the right of a small, walled plantation of mixed trees. Go on to pass the right end of a row of straggly trees, once a hedge, to climb a stile at the end of the wall coming down from the left. Stroll across the next pasture to the edge of fenced woodland. Walk left, as directed by the waymark, to descend through the trees to cross a wooden footbridge. Climb out of the gill on a short muddy track to the edge of a pasture.

With your back to the gill head straight across the pasture to a stile in the hedge, just behind a telegraph pole. Go on over the next pasture to pass through a gate. Bear right and wind round in front of ruined 17th-century Park Style farmhouse. ◄ Carry on along the track now lined with splendid beech trees.

This was one of two entrances into the Leagram Park Estate, where deer were hunted in the Forest of Bowland.

A short way past the trees you have another fine view of the Bleas-dale Fells to the

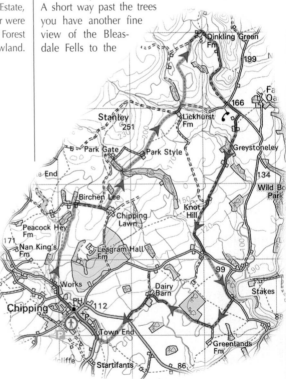

158

*Gate stoop near Dinkling Green*

left and also, to the right, Pendle Hill and Longridge Fell. Remain on the farm track as it passes through a gate on the right and continue on down it until you reach a track to Lickhurst Farm.

Beyond the gate at the foot of the track turn right and, just before the farm buildings, turn left to descend a narrow metalled road. Where the way turns sharp right, go ahead to cross the beck on a footbridge. Walk up the slope ahead to climb a stile. Continue ahead past two 'stranded' gateposts and go on winding left around the foot of a hillock on your right to pass through a gateless gap (gate on the ground at the time of writing). Wind left for a few steps to pass through two stone gateposts, or 'stoops', then descend left of a pond, remaining beside the hedge on your left, to reach a stile in the corner of the pasture.

Beyond, turn right and walk to the left side of a wet track to pass through a gate. Stroll on past (but not through) another pair of old gate stoops – here you can still see the holes and slots for the poles that formed the gate, and also the mason's benchmark. Very soon the

*Restored limekiln at Knot Barn*

path becomes a good track and passes through another gate. Continue to a T-junction of tracks where you turn right to walk into the charming hamlet of Dinkling Green.

As you follow the waymark directing you forward, look for a carved stone head above the doorway of a barn on the left. Also on the left is a barn that was once the hamlet's schoolhouse. To the right another barn once housed a chapel. Beyond, down on the far right, is a tiny 17th-century house. When you can drag yourself away from this lovely spot, walk on along the lane, which bears right, to pass below three fine rounded limestone knolls, Long Knots. Enjoy this pleasing way with its fine view of the fells. At the end of the access lane cross the road and walk on along a continuing lane. After a short distance take the signed bridleway on the right leading to Higher Greystoneley, where several barns have been converted to housing.

Carry on along the track and then descend a rather slippery way through woodland. As you near a ford over the beck, take a narrow path to the right to come to a footbridge. Once across turn left to regain the main track, and climb steadily to Lower Greystoneley before stepping out along the track to pass Knot Barn, another fine conversion.

## LIMEKILN

Just beyond Knot Barn make a short detour right to see a splendidly restored limekiln. You can go inside the large gates to see where workers placed alternating layers of limestone and coal or charcoal. As the fuel burned, the limestone turned into lime. This was added to the soil to neutralise the acidity common to areas of high rainfall. Lime was also used to make mortar and whitewash, and cements for buildings and pavements.

Return to the main track and stroll on to where it ends at a road. Cross and climb the stile opposite. Stroll down the pasture, keeping beside the hedge on your right, to take a stile onto a lane. Walk on for 300 metres then turn right onto a signposted track for 400 metres until the track turns left towards a farm. Here turn right (a post but no waymark) under a tall alder to take a raised grassy trod. Walk on to go through the left of two gates and continue beside the deciduous wood on your right.

Halfway along the wood the distinct track drifts away from the trees and carries on to the aptly named Dairy Barn farm. Wind left in front of the farmhouse and at a T-junction of tracks turn left and walk the access track to the road. Cross and take the signposted stile opposite. Continue ahead over rather rough pasture, keeping parallel with the hedge to your right. Climb a stile and continue on to take a rather battered footbridge over a stream. Turn right to walk parallel with a fence and cross the stone bridge over the beck into Windy Street in Chipping, then turn right. Walk on to pass John Brabin's old school and the almshouses on the right. The date over the ancient studded door of his old home is 1668. Then head towards the church, and turn left and then right to return to the car park.

# WALK 32

## Longridge Fell

| | |
|---|---|
| **Distance** | 9.8km (6 miles) |
| **Time** | 3 hours |
| **Terrain** | Good tracks over the moor; distinct, well-waymarked concessionary paths through the forest, some of which can be muddy after rain |
| **Maps** | OS Explorer OL41 and 287 |

Park in the car park at the top of Jeffrey Hill, grid ref 639403. This is reached by following the signs for Longridge Golf Course clubhouse and continuing on the narrow road where it climbs for about 1.5km (nearly 1 mile) before dropping a little to pass Cardwell House. Here turn right and the car park lies on the left.

From Spire Hill (350m (1155ft)) on Longridge Fell you look down on the wide, lush Vale of Chipping, through which flows the River Hodder. Sheltering this lovely pastoral valley and dominating the view are the Bleasdale Fells, with Parlick almost hiding the lovely curve of Blindhurst Fell, but not high enough to obscure the cairn way up on the summit of Fair Snape Fell. In the distance to the west you can glimpse the sea washing the Fylde coast.

This is a most enjoyable walk of contrasts, first across moorland and then through an attractive forest using well-waymarked paths and tracks.

Head for the nearby kissing gate, which gives access to the signposted concessionary path across the moor. From this waymarked path the walker has spectacular views over the Vale of Chipping to the long, dramatic ridge of the Bleasdale Fells. The path leads to the rim of the hill and joins a wider way where you turn right. Continue on to cross a small stream, then follow the waymarked path just beyond as it winds right to carry on across the moor and come to a wall with Longridge Fell forest beyond.

Turn left and keep beside the wall on your right. Ignore any left turns and carry on along the distinct way, heather moor stretching away to your left. Carry on climbing gently until you reach the trig point on Spire Hill, where you may want to linger to enjoy the superb view. Then climb

'Throughs' in a fell wall

the steps (known as 'throughs') embedded in the wall to join a wide ride between the wall and the fenced woodland. Turn left and walk on through heather to reach a concessionary stile through the fence.

Then, in great contrast with your walk over the open moorland, go ahead along a stony path through mixed conifers until you reach a post with two waymarks, both directing your right. Very soon you join a wide forest road where you turn right. Ignore the signed footpath going off left and continue steadily downhill. At the T-junction turn left and almost immediately take a footpath going off right. This continues through an open area and then enters the forest again.

Continue on an embanked path that runs along the middle of a wide ride with mixed woodland on either side. Eventually the forest ends on your left and you can see the wide open pastures about Green Thorn farm. Here go ahead, still on the path as directed by the waymark, to walk just inside the edge of the plantation that stretches away on your right. Then you enter woodland on both sides of the path, passing under some magnificent ancient beeches. Carry on until you reach a kissing gate onto Old Clitheroe Road.

Do not join the road, but turn right to follow a concessionary path that runs through deciduous woodland beside the wall of the road. Continue along the way to pass a quarry now charmingly colonised by vegetation. Keep going until you reach a wide forest track where you turn right.

Climb easily through the trees, ignoring a left turn and going on up the rising way. Follow it as directed by the waymark as it does eventually turn left. Keep on along the track, and continue where it narrows to a path that winds left along the top side of a clearing and goes on to the forest edge and the now familiar wall. Climb over the steps embedded in the wall to enjoy once again the fine view of the distant fells.

Turn left and walk beside the wall until you are parallel with the end of the trees on your right. Here turn right to walk the path across the moor used earlier. Cross

*Longridge Fell*

the little stream and continue on along the rim of Jeffrey Hill, being sure not to miss the waymarked concessionary path to the left that takes you back to the car park.

# WALK 33

## *Ribchester*

| | |
|---|---|
| **Distance** | 9km (5½ miles) |
| **Time** | 3 hours |
| **Terrain** | Easy walking along good tracks for much of the way |
| **Maps** | OS Explorer 287 |

Park in the large pay-and-display car park, grid ref 651353, reached by a signposted turn off Church Street. Walk left out of the parking area and then right along Church Street. As you go look for the 18th-century

The village of Ribchester is encircled by gently rolling hills and sits in a curve of the River Ribble, from which it takes its name. Travellers used to cross the river here – a dangerous exploit because it is wide and it surges – but now swallows and house martins are more likely to be found enjoying the spot, delighting in the profusion of insects over its waters on a summer's day. Beneath the village are the remains of a Roman fort, Bremetannacum, built some time around AD80, and which housed 500 soldiers. Part of the fort lies under the churchyard of the parish church, which is partly 13th century, and just outside its gates is the Roman museum.

cottages that once housed handloom weavers, particularly those opposite the White Bull. The inn has a fine canopy supported by columns and bearing a striking carved wooden bull. Continue on for your first view of the swift-flowing River Ribble – when the level is low you can just spot the ford that the Romans and other travellers crossed. Turn right to walk the Ribble Way, continuing past the access road to the museum and the church. A short distance along follow the track that winds away from the river to pass through a farmyard.

*The White Bull inn, Ribchester*

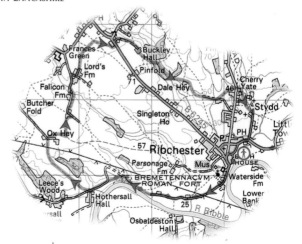

Stride the hedged track out into the quiet Lancashire countryside. Eventually to your left you can see, on the far bank of the river – here hidden from view by a fold in the pastures – Osbaldeston Hall, a majestic Elizabethan house. Carry on ahead, ignoring any right or left turns, soon to come closer to the river once more, from where curlews call.

Beyond the next stile climb a path that leads into woodland, with ash and sycamore covering the steep slope as it drops down to the river. Emerge from the trees and follow the path above gorse scrub. From here enjoy the view of the curving river, flowing through green pastures. Descend gently to go through a gate into a wide green track fenced on both sides, and then walk on to pass gracious Hothersall Hall, rebuilt in 1856. Beyond, high on a building, a stone plaque carries the initials T. H. and the date 1695, all that remains of the original manor house.

Follow the Ribble Way sign to ascend the concrete access track and come to a cross of tracks. Here turn right to climb the reinforced track, and at the top continue ahead over a vast pasture to a gate in the left corner. Walk ahead to the next gate in the far right corner, which gives access to a fenced grassy trod, and at its end continue ahead along a hedged, tarmacked lane. At the T-junction ignore the turn right and wind left to stand in front of Ox Hey. Take the gate opposite the dwelling and wind right along a wide, waymarked bridleway to just beyond the next waymarked gate.

Here leave the bridleway and turn left to walk beside the fence on the left to a sturdy footbridge over a narrow gutter. Follow the gutter left and then bear right. Pass between a marl pit and the hedge, and then strike right of Eatoughs Farm to a gate with a difficult catch (it is easier if you lift the gate) in the right corner up against the fence. This gives access to a hedged track where you turn left. Climb the stile and follow the track to take another going off right, opposite the vehicle access track to Eatoughs Farm.

Carry on along the track, which soon becomes metalled, following it where it drops down a steep slope shaded by tall trees. Pass the track on the left to Falicon Farm and continue past two more dwellings on your right, and then turn right into another track which you leave after a few steps to walk left into the yard of Lord's Farm. Continue on, following the waymarks, to pass between farm buildings and then through gates into a pasture with a fence on your right. Walk ahead to climb

*The River Ribble*

the next stile and press on through a second pasture with the fence to your left. Beyond the next stile ignore the waymarked route and go ahead beside the hedge on your left to climb a stile in the corner. Next, head diagonally right across another pasture to a rickety stile in the hedgerow. Beyond, follow the yellow-topped posts leading diagonally left to a stile into the garden of a house. Continue through gates onto Preston Road, which you cross, and then walk left and almost immediately take the signposted track on your right.

Stride yet another long track with pleasing views across the pastures to pass in front of fine Buckley Hall. Most of the original hall was pulled down in 1895 and the present dwelling was once part of the north wing. Beyond, head across a pasture towards a tall red disk below which is a stile in the corner of Buckley Wood. Drop left down the stepped slope through the woodland to cross the footbridge over Boyce's Brook into a secluded grassy hollow beside the stream. Follow the brook downstream to a footbridge over a feeder stream, then carry on along the path to ascend the slope through gorse and climb a stile over a fence with a white post beyond. Walk right to the next white post and then follow more posts to pass to the left of Ashmoor House. Beyond, follow the posts to a stile through the hedge on the right and then walk left to join its access track.

Head on along the track, ignoring a footpath going off right, and carry on towards Boyce's Farm. At the end of the second barn and before the farmhouse, turn left to climb the stile in the corner of the fence. Keep to the left of a pond and then continue to a footbridge at the left end of a row of willows. Beyond, climb the slope and continue ahead to a stile to Stonygate Lane, opposite Cherry Yate, which has an attractive staircase window. Look for the name and datestone, 1684, set in the wall of the house.

Cross the lane, turn left and take the signposted stile on the right. Drop diagonally right to cross a small stream and continue to a gate into Stydd Manor farm. A stone over its front door carries the date 1698. Pass through another gate and walk towards lovely old Stydd church, with its Norman doorway and north-facing windows. Continue on to pass Stydd almshouses, endowed for Catholic women in 1726 by John Shireburn.

Carry on to Stone Bridge on Blackburn Road, turn right and walk into Ribchester – with time left to explore the charming village.

# WALK 34

## Lytham

| | |
|---|---|
| **Distance** | 12km (7½ miles) |
| **Time** | 3–4 hours |
| **Terrain** | Easy walking all the way |
| **Maps** | OS Explorer 286 |

This walk starts from the car park on the Green behind Lytham's lifeboat station, grid ref 366269. From here you can see immediately the extensive stretches of manicured grass on either side of the parking area. A splendid 19th-century windmill, Lytham's much-loved landmark, stands on the Green just to the east. It was built by the Squire of Lytham in 1805 on an area known as Lytham Marshland and leased to a Mr Cookson for a rent of 7 shillings (35p) a year. Used as a cornmill, a gas engine was installed for when the weather was calm. It was in constant use and served a wide area. Beside the windmill nestles the lifeboat house, built in 1863 and constructed mainly from sea cobbles. The town's popularity as a holiday resort increased with the arrival of the railway, and visitors were drawn to the working cornmill as they walked along the Green.

The walk takes you along the promenade and then, after a little road walking, out along embankments from where you overlook the Ribble Marshes, the flats teeming with birdlife. The return is made across pastures and along quiet lanes through the fertile flat lands of the Fylde coastal plain. Finally you reach Lytham, hopefully with time on your hands to enjoy this solidly handsome town of 18th-century elegance.

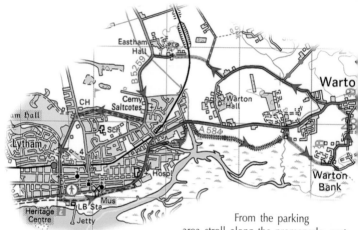

From the parking area stroll along the promenade, part of the Lancashire Coastal Way, to pass the windmill, the lifeboat house and the toilets, and with a fine view of the Welsh mountains on a clear day. At the end of the promenade join the A584 Lytham road and continue right for just under 800 metres (½ mile) until you have crossed the Craving Dock redbrick road bridge. Just beyond a signpost directs you right to walk a distinct path beside a creek.

Follow the path on and on, passing through a waymarked boatyard and carrying on to join the main road. Turn right and in a few steps take the signposted way on the right to join the embankment and stroll the airy way, the grassy Ribble marshland stretching away to the right and farmland to the left.

Follow the path for about 1.5km (nearly 1 mile) and then go with it as it winds inland. Climb a stile and walk an overgrown path beside a brook to join the A584 once more. Turn right, cross the bridge and turn right again and follow the way to return to the embankment. Continue along the stiled way for 800 metres (½ mile), descending from it just before two cottages. Beyond, wind left on a metalled road, Warton Bank. Continue along this winding way for another 800 metres (½ mile), and where

*Windmill at Lytham*

the road turns sharply right take the signposted ladderstile in the hedge on the left. Walk a few steps to pass through a wooden arch, and then head across the large pasture beyond to the last house on the left. A short distance further left, along a hedge, take the footbridge, deep in the hedge, over a brook. Walk up an alleyway to join the main road and cross.

Turn left, walk on, and between a car-washing station and a petrol station turn right into West End Lane. After a short distance the houses cease and you continue along the quiet hedged way with pastures on either side. Ignore the turn on the right and head on along Lodge Lane. Once past Carr Farm take the signposted bridleway on the right that passes through fields. Where the track winds

*Drainage dyke near Lytham*

right, take the easy-to-miss stile on the left. Walk up beside the hedge on your right and past a stranded stile to come to the side of the railway line. Cross with care and go ahead for a few steps.

Turn left through a large gate (or gateway if the gate is open) and immediately walk right to join a path hidden by a huge lime tree. Stride on along the edge of a scrubby hedgerow to your left, with Eastham Hall caravan site beyond a fence on the right. At the end of the path join an access road and turn left to join Saltcotes Road, where you walk left. Cross the road bridge over a dyke and carry on along the narrow pavement. Pass Saltcotes Catholic Cemetery, and just before the road junction cross over and turn into a wide track which passes through a broad belt of lofty deciduous woodland. At its end cross Ballam Road with care and turn left to walk with a triangle of grass to your left. Carry on into Lytham and walk past the shops and cafés and through pedestrian areas to reach the Green and the car park behind the lifeboat station.

# WALK 35

## *Croston and the Rufford branch of the Leeds–Liverpool Canal*

| | |
|---|---|
| **Distance** | 13km (8 miles) |
| **Time** | 4 hours |
| **Terrain** | Easy, level walking, though field paths can be muddy; if the River Douglas is abnormally high you may not be able to pass under the railway bridge and will have to follow the alternative route described |
| **Maps** | OS Explorer 285 |

It is possible to park in Croston's surgery car park, grid ref 489186, from 7pm Wednesday to 7pm on Sunday. At any other time you will have to use street parking. From the

The name Croston means the 'town of the cross'. Today's village cross was erected in 1950 on small steps in cobbled Church Street, an attractive terrace of cottages that frames the late-Gothic Church of St Michael and All Angels, with its out-of-line tower. To the right of the church stands the 14th-century school, licensed by John of Gaunt, Duke of Lancaster. Close by the picturesque cobbled Town Bridge, built in 1682, crosses the River Yarrow. West of the village this river joins the River Lostock and together their waters surge on to unite with the River Douglas. Well-maintained embankments confine these rivers as they pass through the flat and intensively farmed west Lancashire plain, where huge fields of cereals grow on what were once unproductive mosses, reclaimed during the 18th and 19th centuries.

parking area walk left to pass the Lord Nelson pub on the left (there are a few parking bays here) and then the Wheatsheaf on the right. Beyond the latter turn right to walk west along the A581. Cross the road bridge over the river and then the bridge over the railway. Carry on along the narrow pavement, and once level with the discreet sewage works climb the embankment and walk on the raised way (the River Yarrow flows to your right). Follow the route where it winds left at the confluence of the Lostock and the Yarrow.

Stride on along the continuing embankment, still with the Yarrow to your right. Enjoy the ducks on the water, and go on to pass a few scattered trees with the flat land stretching away on either side. Then wind left where the river joins the Douglas, remaining on the delightful embankment for about 800 metres (nearly ½ mile) to join the A581 again.

Turn right and cross Great Hanging Bridge with care – it is busy, narrow and has no pavement – then take the signposted stiled footpath on the left. This continues for about 1.7km (more than 1 mile) along another high embankment with the River Douglas on your left. The last stile gives access to a small grassy area close to the river and a railway bridge. Descend the slope to take a railed footbridge with a concrete base and go under the railway bridge. Next, climb a small slope and walk on over a

manicured grassy way beside a 'fishing pond' on your right to join Station Road by a squeeze stile.

If the river is abnormally high and you cannot pass under the railway bridge, you will have to return over the stile and take now, on your left, a farm gate, walk ahead over pastures to go through a gate onto the towpath and turn right to walk a few steps to see Rufford Old Hall on the other side of the canal. Return back along the canal to the road. Turn left, go over the level crossing and then cross White Bridge over the River Douglas.

Immediately beyond, turn left into a wide track and pass an Environment Agency building. Stride on along the sturdy track as it leads out into fields to cross a foot-bridge, then carry on to pass through a derelict wall. Ignore a rather rough plank bridge on the left and go on, following the continuing little path that runs along the edge of the field on the right with a ditch on the left. Wind round the corner of the field to pass a waymark and continue ahead to the next corner, where you turn right to walk along the edge of another field. At the next waymark go ahead as directed until you reach a waymarked footbridge – here you turn left and continue ahead to eventually reach Sumner's Farm. Bear a few steps right and then stride left along leafy Carr Lane, carrying on through the flat pastures to arrive at the pack-horse bridge over the River Yarrow. Cross and bear right and then right again into Church Street to visit the church and its surrounds. Then return to the A581 and turn left to walk on with the River Yarrow, flanked with high walls, to your left. A short way along cross the road and turn right in front of the Lord Nelson to reach the car park.

*Great Hanging Bridge near Croston*

*Church and old grammar school, Croston*

# WALK 36

## *Martin Mere and Mere Sands Wood*

| | |
|---|---|
| **Distance** | 9km (5½ miles) |
| **Time** | 3 hours |
| **Terrain** | Easy walking all the way |
| **Maps** | OS Explorer 285 |

The Martin Mere Wildfowl Centre lies 9.5km (6 miles) north of Ormskirk and 16km (10 miles) southeast of Southport. Leave your car in the car park, grid ref 433144, and walk through the coach park to join a footpath passing through birch, the busy road to your left. When the path decants you onto the roadside at Fish Lane, cross and continue on along the pavement. Where it becomes Tarlscough Lane carry on until the pavement runs out, then cross again and walk the pavement on the

Martin Mere is a large lake that once covered approximately 40 sq km (15 sq miles). Over the centuries low-lying land, much of it below sea level, was gradually drained for agriculture, but a small portion was never successfully reclaimed and in 1972 the Wildfowl and Wetlands Trust bought it and established a centre here, which is where the walk begins. It continues to Mere Sands Wood Nature Reserve, which is owned and managed by the Lancashire Wildlife Trust. The nature reserve stands on layered sand and peat. Between 1974 and 1982 the sand was extensively quarried for glass making, and then the extraction companies landscaped the site and created the nature reserve.

other side for a short distance further until it also runs out. Here cross the road again to walk Curlew Lane, a left turn off the main road which takes you through vast flat acres composed in winter of dark-brown peaty-sandy soil and in summer huge areas of vegetables. The vista is nearly treeless and hedgeless.

Ignoring all footpaths on both sides, go along Curlew Lane, where in season workers gather a huge crop of cabbages from the almost-black soil. Follow the narrow lane and continue as it swings right and becomes Tootle Lane. Pass Mere End farm, and a short way beyond take the signposted track on the left leading to a footbridge over Rufford Boundary Sluice, which you cross. Turn right to walk through beech and rhododendrons, part of woodland planted in the mid-19th century by Lord Hesketh.

180

*Small cottage in vast acres of arable land, Martin Mere*

Just before the end of the wood turn left to follow the very good track through deciduous woodland, passing through birch and Scots pine, where you might see a red squirrel. To the left a path edged with trees leads to the Cyril Gibbons Hide, where you might spot coot, gold-eneye, shoveller and pochard. Return to the main track and carry on to the visitor centre (there are toilets here). Leading from the visitor centre through a picnic site is a path to the Lancaster Hide, from where there is a splendid view of the Scrape, a series of connected lakes formed from sand quarrying in the 1970s. Close to the hide you might spot a bevy of reed buntings.

Retrace your steps to take the first turn on your right through the woodland to stand on End Lake platform. At the right time of year courting grebes are often seen here. Press on along the main path as it winds right and comes to the well-signed Rufford Hide. From here there is a magnificent view of Twin Island and an extensive stretch of water that is generally a birdwatcher's delight. A little further on is the Redwing Hide, also a good viewing point for the lake. Perhaps here you might see a flash of petrol blue, revealing a kingfisher. Rejoin the path and turn right to cross another bridge.

Wind on round the western side of the wildfowl centre, continuing to the northern corner where a signpost directs you towards Holmeswood village. Turn left out of the trees and then almost immediately right along a wide track to join the road – this may be busy, with rather fast traffic.

Cross the road and walk the pavement for a few metres, and then cross again to take the first left turn, Sandy Lane. Follow the road as it winds right, and at its end go through a gate beside a padlocked farm gate. Walk ahead to continue along a grassy trod, a hedge on one side and a fence on the other, to come to a tall waymark directing you left through a tall, solid gate into the garden of a house. Walk ahead and then turn right to keep right of the conservatory (the waymarks directing you through the garden are high on the wall). At the end of the conservatory go ahead to another solid gate through a fence almost hidden by tall bushes. Beyond the gate follow a winding fenced ginnel that eventually leads you to a road where you turn right to join Sandy Way. Turn left to continue along the lane, which eventually leads out into flat arable land once again.

Where the lane turns sharp left, walk on ahead over the field with a hawthorn hedge to the right and go over a footbridge over a dyke. Beyond, walk half right across the land to a signposted stile, then turn left and continue a few steps to a board carrying an arrow and a request that you keep to the path. Walk in the direction of the arrow along a wide, tractor-wheel-marked track to a raised track traversing left, a ditch beside it on your right. At the end of the track and the dyke bear right and stroll another very pleasing grassy track towards a small brick cottage. Carry on past it and then wind right to join Fish Lane.

Turn right, and a short distance along cross the road to take the footpath, the same one taken earlier to reach the wildfowl centre. The centre is open daily from 9.30am to 5.30pm in summer, 4.00pm in winter. It is closed on 24 and 25 December. If you have timed your walk well you will still be able to see the flamingos, the

many and varied ducks, and in winter watch the comings and goings of a huge number of Bewick's and whooper swans. You will find much to do and see and there is a small restaurant. All admission money goes directly to conserving wetland environments. Don't forget your binoculars!

*Whoopers feeding time, Martin Mere*

## WALK 37

### *Parbold and the Leeds–Liverpool Canal*

| | |
|---|---|
| **Distance** | 9.5km (6 miles) |
| **Time** | 3–4 hours |
| **Terrain** | Easy walking all the way; a gently rising path takes you up on to Parbold Hill; the towpath is a joy to walk |
| **Maps** | OS Explorer 285 |

Parbold Hill (121m (400ft)), the most westerly outlier of the Pennines, rises above the low-lying land of west Lancashire. It is through this flat land that the Leeds–Liverpool Canal has been cut. The walk starts along the canal but soon leaves it and climbs gently to the hill, passing through fertile pastures on the way and returning along the canalside from Appley Bridge to Parbold, a peaceful stretch of towpath. At the beginning of the walk, at Parbold, look for the stump of an old windmill. Much flour was milled in the village, which had another mill that stood on the far bank of the canal, but which has been replaced by elegant town houses.

The Leeds–Liverpool, Britain's longest canal, was constructed to provide a trans-Pennine waterway linking the emergent industrial towns in Yorkshire and Lancashire with the North American market via Liverpool. Work began at the same time from both ends, in Leeds and Liverpool, after the first Canal Act was passed in 1770.

There is a small parking area on the northwest side of Parbold canal bridge no 37, grid ref 494105. If it is full continue a short way west along the village main street and park behind a row of shops on the right side of the road (A5209). Failing that, there is more parking further along the main road outside the village hall, just off a left turn named the Green.

Wherever you have parked, return to cross Parbold Bridge and descend left to join the towpath with the waterway to your left. Walk on the pleasing way, with a charming view to the left of the parish church. Here look for a short cut of water on the far side of the canal – this was meant to be the start of a link to the River Ribble, but it remained just a short cut. Go on to pass under the A5209 road bridge and carry on until you can cross the waterway by picturesque cobbled bridge no 39.

Carry on ahead along the continuing shady lane to reach a T-junction. Cross and bear slightly right to take a stile immediately on the left onto a path that runs up beside the fence of the last of a row of houses. Soon the path climbs steadily up into pastures from where you should pause and look back for a fine view over south Lancashire. Then go on up to climb a stile onto the busy

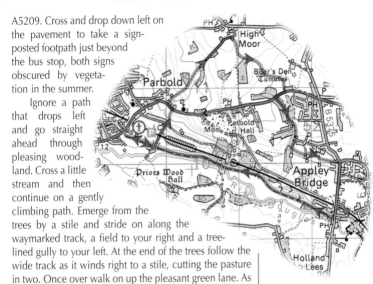

A5209. Cross and drop down left on the pavement to take a sign-posted footpath just beyond the bus stop, both signs obscured by vegetation in the summer.

Ignore a path that drops left and go straight ahead through pleasing woodland. Cross a little stream and then continue on a gently climbing path. Emerge from the trees by a stile and stride on along the waymarked track, a field to your right and a tree-lined gully to your left. At the end of the trees follow the wide track as it winds right to a stile, cutting the pasture in two. Once over walk on up the pleasant green lane. As you near Bowling Green House Farm, the highest part of this walk, bear right along the access track shaded by forest trees. Parbold Hill, 27m higher than Bowling Green House Farm, lies a mile northeast and can be reached by footpaths.

Where the road turns left and there is a footpath sign, turn sharp right to walk a hedged green lane with vast pastures on either side and fine views over to the Pennines. Pass two small copses on your left, and at a Y-junction of grassy trods take the left branch to go on past a small pool surrounded by alders. Walk on towards a woodland and bear left alongside its edge. Go over two stiles and continue on down through woodland, crossing a footbridge and bearing left to carry on along a wet area. Then climb a stile out of the trees and walk on with a wall to the left. Follow the path as it winds round the far edge of the large field to join a layby on the A5209.

Turn right and join the road, remaining on the pavement for a few metres before crossing opposite a board welcoming you to Fairy Glen. This is an idyllic corner,

*Shady footpath on the way to Parbold Hill*

where fine trees shadow Sprodley Brook as it dances through its ravine and much work has been done to put in footbridges and excellent paths. Just off the road turn left to take a stepped path that drops down beside the brook on your left. Go on down the easy path with the brook now appearing on your right. Don't cross the next footbridge but descend steps that take you below huge, tree-clad sandstone crags. Cross the next footbridge and look back to see a pretty waterfall before walking on a slightly raised path with a stream on either side. Ignore the steep steps down to the right and climb gently left to a track where you turn right to leave the glen.

After 50 metres take a stile on the left hidden by a hedge and just before a gate to a farm. Stride the continuing footpath beside a hedge on your right and go through a gap in the hedge ahead to cross a lane and climb the steps opposite. Walk ahead to another stile and then on across the middle of a field to a lane. Turn right for 20 metres and then take the footpath left to continue along a grassy way, in the same general direction, to Appley Lane North, where you turn right.

Descend the B5375, cross the bridge over the railway and press on over canal bridge no 42. Beyond, drop down right to the towpath, go past some cottages and continue out into the rolling Lancashire countryside. Dawdle past a canal lock with deciduous woodland on the opposite bank. Here be alert for a flash of petrol blue when a kingfisher darts above the waterway. Stride on along the towpath, passing under and beside bridges until you reach Parbold. Climb a slope to join the road and turn right to return to the place where you have parked.

*The Leeds–Liverpool Canal*

# WALK 38

## *Darwen Moor, Jubilee Tower and the Witton Weavers Way*

| | |
|---|---|
| **Distance** | 13km (8 miles) |
| **Time** | 4–5 hours |
| **Terrain** | A challenging walk in parts, but on generally good paths; some muddy patches on moorland sections; steady climb to the Jubilee Tower on Darwen Hill; after rain or a heavy dew walkers might need to wear waterproof trousers or gaiters to protect them from the wet vegetation, particularly heather, that hangs over many of the paths that have sunk below ground level after years of use |
| **Maps** | OS Explorer 287 |

The tower on Darwen Hill was built in 1897 to celebrate Queen Victoria's diamond jubilee. It also celebrated the opening of Darwen Moor to the public after a long fight for access. Inside the tower wide, shallow steps lead to an outside walled parapet, and more steps lead to a door giving access to another parapet. From the tower you might be able to spot Snowdonia and Great Orme's Head, with the Irish Sea beyond, and on a clear day the Isle of Man can be seen. There is also a splendid view of Darwen and its 100-metre (330ft) tall India Mill chimney, modelled on the style of a Venetian campanile. Taking 14 years to complete at a cost of £14,000, it was opened in 1868. In recent years peregrine falcons have successfully nested on the chimney.

The long-distance Witton Weavers Way (WWW) is made up of four circular walks predominantly within the west Pennine moors. The tracks over Darwen Moor and the plateau were mostly built by miners to get to the pits where poor-grade coal was mined for more than 300 years.

Park in the back car park at Roddlesworth Information Centre, grid ref 665215 (there are toilets here). This is

next to the Royal Arms at the top of the hill close to the hamlet of Ryal Fold. Return to the road and turn left and then left again into Hollinshead Terrace, a row of cottages built for people who worked at the one-time Tockholes cotton mill. Turn right immediately before the cottages to pass through a gate. Climb a cobbled track ahead, waymarked with small stone pillars engraved with an outline of the Jubilee Tower. As you ascend look left for a good view of, first, Earnsdale Reservoir in its valley, then Sunnyhurst Hey Reservoir set in hilly pastures. Ahead stands Beacon Hill.

Carry on up the gated track into mixed deciduous woodland where very soon the path winds left to a stile. Beyond, continue on the path as it swings left and then take the narrower track on the right that swings back above the track just walked. Climb steadily upwards,

*Jubilee Tower from Darwen Moor*

following the track as it veers left to a 'stranded' stile at the top of the slope. Walk ahead along the 'rim' of the slopes to a Y-junction where you take the right branch to come to the foot of the tower. (Where you start your ascent after leaving the trees there are various paths and several stiles, which can be bewildering, but the best path to follow is the one identified by the stone markers.)

Spend time at the tower, enjoying the view and the majestic shape of the construction, and then wind halfway round it to join the Witton Weavers Way and head south over Darwen Moor. From here you can look down on the town of Darwen – on the nearest edge of the town stands India Mill, with its tall chimney. The path is clearly waymarked with the WWW logo both here and as it crosses the rather bleak moor, where a scattering of deciduous trees has been planted. At the Y-junction of paths take the left branch and carry on as the way takes you along the edge of steep grassy slopes dropping down to your left. Notice the seats that have been placed beside the path for walkers to pause and enjoy the superb views.

The WWW path, wet in places but always distinct, takes you on and on until you descend quite steeply to a narrow metalled lane. Turn right and very soon the way

*Looking down on India Mill and chimney, Darwen*

winds left and climbs steeply, with a house above you to the right and a steep gully to the left through which flows Duckshaw Brook. Where the lane turns right and the crash barrier starts take an easy-to-miss WWW path going off left. This continues ahead through heather and along roughly the same contour. Cross a footbridge and stroll on to climb a stile, then go on to negotiate a rather wet hollow beyond which the path improves.

Carry on along the WWW, with a fence beside you, and enjoy the vast views into the distance and the heather moorland sweeping up on the right. Climb an awkward stile to stride a grassy sward, then all too soon you need to climb another stile with boggy patches on both sides. Stroll on along the improving way through an open area planted with a great variety of trees, the path following the posts of an old fence, before leaving by a stile out onto the moorland.

Climb ahead for a few steps and then walk left over the pathless pasture, diverging slightly right away from the mature woodland on your left. Cross a track, then a raised area over a pipeline and then look ahead to the waymarked stile to the right of the corner where two walls meet. Descend the pasture beyond, very slightly left and towards a solitary tree close beside the ruined foundations of an old farm – look for the cobbled area beside it. Descend the grassy slope to cross a good stile over a fence and then head on down to take the next stile onto a wide reinforced track.

Turn right to begin a steady climb through lonely Cadshaw Valley with Turton Moor to your left. Pass the ruin of Top o' th' Brow farm and notice the beautifully constructed culvert to your left, carrying water from the stream above. ◄ Continue climbing the gated reinforced way for about 1.5km (nearly 1 mile). Once out of the valley the now grassy way continues through rolling moorland as it gradually winds west.

Continue on to a signpost and go through a kissing gate. Walk on to pass through the next gate and then begin your descent to the valley below. Remain on the path as it nears the valley bottom and then swing right to

In the 19th century 200 people lived and worked in the valley before the land was taken over by Liverpool Corporation for water supply works.

## HOLLINSHEAD HALL

Hollinshead Hall was the manor house of nearby Tockholes, whose last owner, Eccles Shorrock, allowed the 18th- and 19th-century buildings to fall into disrepair. The site was demolished in 1911 by Liverpool Corporation, who needed the stone to build a wall to keep sheep out of the newly planted woods around Roddlesworth Reservoir. Look right as you pass the ruins to see, under trees, the wellhouse. Five springs of water meet here and legend says that they have healing properties for eyes.

walk on. Do not join the road, but turn right to pass through a gate and walk left. The gate gives access to a pleasant concessionary path that takes you over a pasture and beside beech woodland, bypassing for 350 metres what can be a busy road.

Rejoin the road by a gate, cross over and go through another gate. Walk on along a delectable path that winds right and comes to a clearing where once stood **Hollinshead Hall**.

Go on to follow the walled way as it winds right to pass the ornate old gateposts which once marked the entrance to the defunct hall. Climb steadily beside pleasing woodland and go through a gate, ignoring the place where the track now turns right. Descend a wide track as it passes through more deciduous woodland, ignoring too the waymarked left turn and going on under an avenue of beech. Cross the footbridge and take the iron kissing gate to walk with the River Roddlesworth to your right. Look for the dramatic sandstone cliffs on the far side of the river.

Cross a footbridge, climb steps and carry on to join a path coming in on your left. Go past a seat, wind on to descend more steps and walk on close to the river once more. Go past the waymark, cross the river and at the three-armed signpost turn right to reach a main track and another signpost. Cross the track and continue climbing a narrow way to ascend two sets of steps. This brings you out of the woodland at the front of the Royal Arms. Turn right and then left to return to the information centre.

# WALK 39

## *Thieveley Pike, Cliviger Gorge*

| | |
|---|---|
| **Distance** | 10.5km (6½ miles) |
| **Time** | 3–4 hours |
| **Terrain** | The climb to the trig point on Thieveley Pike is a delight, quite high but well contoured except for the first 50 metres; the zigzagging path up onto the moorland opposite is not to be missed, but choose a good day – finding your way across Heald Moor in the mist should be avoided |
| **Maps** | OS Explorer OL21 |

This up-and-down-several-times walk starts from Holme Chapel, a linear village set snugly near the brow of the road through the magnificent Cliviger Gorge. Water from the high moorland slopes percolates down to the valley bottom to form both the Lancashire and Yorkshire Calder rivers. Dr TD Whitaker, an 18th-century historian, was a member of the family that lived for several generations at Holme Chapel and he planted many of the woodland trees beside which you stroll at the start of the walk. Today, as a Millennium project, hundreds more trees have been planted on the scars of opencast mine workings. This mixed deciduous woodland has been named Burnley Wood and is part of the Forest of Burnley. Overlooking all is Thieveley Pike (449m (1470ft)), the highest point of the walk.

Holme Chapel lies 5km (3 miles) southeast of Burnley on the A646. Park in the large layby, grid ref 926396, 400 metres southeast of the linear settlement. Walk back on the pavement towards the village and cross with care to take the first signposted track, an acute left turn, off the A646 to pass Pot Ovens farm.

Continue along a walled path to cross a footbridge over a stream and on into Royd Wood. Turn left at the waymark and descend steps to pass an anglers' pond

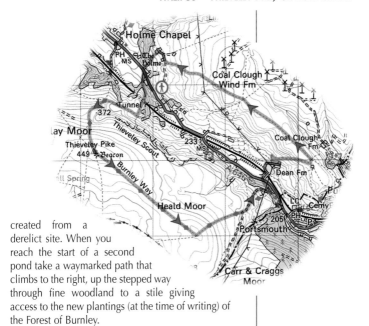

created from a derelict site. When you reach the start of a second pond take a waymarked path that climbs to the right, up the stepped way through fine woodland to a stile giving access to the new plantings (at the time of writing) of the Forest of Burnley.

Carry on up the steep waymarked winding path to the brow. Here turn right along the ridge and go on high above a large grassy hollow which lies at the foot of the great cleft of Dean Scout. Just above the hollow, now planted with trees, is the site of an old lead mine. Pause here for a fine view of the magnificent buttressed side of the gorge, with its many flutings and tiny landslips.

Once beyond the fenced edge of Dean Scout, bear left along a good grassy path, the Burnley Way, indicated by a 'B' waymark and a swift pointing the way with its beak. The path rises easily, well to the left of the rim of the cleft. Follow the distinct way to arrive at a wide track. Pause here to look down at the huge slabby boulders of Eagle Crag, perched precariously on the steep west side of the cleft. Cross the track and go ahead on an easy narrow path over the high moorland to reach the trig point on Thieveley Pike (449m (1470ft)), the site of an ancient beacon. Stand with your back to the trig point and enjoy the view of Pendle Hill to the left with its 'smaller copy', Longridge Fell, further left. Ahead you can spot Boulsworth Hill and below it the reservoirs near Hurst Wood.

Still with your back to the trig point, walk to the right beside the fence to your right. Looking ahead into Yorkshire you can see Stoodley Pike standing bold on the skyline. After a few metres climb the stile over the fence and stride the clear path, the Burnley Way, along the other side, following the way as it steadily moves away from the fence. Continue on over the moorland to pass through a gate in a wall – there is a sign on the gate indicating the South Pennine Packhorse Trail (SPPT). Beyond, where the wall turns away right, go ahead on a narrow path that carries on over featureless Heald Moor. Halfway towards the brow the path becomes indistinct, and after rain the moorland peat holds plenty of water. If you are in doubt about the route, or you have to leave the path, return to it as soon as possible, always aiming for a tall metal pole that supports a simple weather station (an anemometer and so on) on the top of Heald Brow (432m (1431ft)).

Just before the weather station a Burnley Way sign directs you left to go downhill on a good path. Continue easily down and down to climb a stile. Beyond, follow a little path to join a wide gravel track and descend steeply left. At the waymarked T-junction of tracks wind left and then curve right for a very short distance. Watch out for where the track winds sharp left and becomes grassy, well before the first buildings on the edge of the village of Portsmouth. It drops steadily and delightfully through woodland and then levels out before reaching a sign-posted gate to the side of the A646.

Cross with care and go on through a signposted open area to go over a railway bridge. Follow the continuing track as it goes left to wind round a small reservoir, and go on along it as it climbs up to just before the outbuildings of Dean Farm. Wind left to climb again a little to a gate onto a wide grassy trod, part of the SPPT, which turns

back above the gravel track. Continue up the zigzagging way, being careful not to miss where it winds left just before a hawthorn tree, and go on climbing past a large reed-fringed pool. Go through a gate and continue on along this enjoyable route. Wind left by a ruined building, as directed by a prominent waymark, and carry on with a wall and then a fence to your right.

*The Pennine village of Portsmouth*

In front of the next gate an arrow directs you left beside the wall on your right to pass through a gate. Carry on with the wall to your right beyond which there is a wind farm. For much of the way there is a dramatic view of the steep slopes of Cliviger Gorge away to the left. Ignoring a small ladderstile to your right, carry on over a seriously wet patch and then continue to a gate in the corner of two walls.

Beyond, walk on with the wall now to your left until you can climb through it at an awkward waymarked stile. Carry on in the same direction to a waymark on a tall post where you start your descent. Look for the next waymark half left beyond a small ditch. Climb the next stile in a wall, go on through a gateless gap in another wall and head on to the next waymark. Beyond, continue along the rim of the ditch, now to your right, and descend to

*Cliviger Gorge*

stones to cross the water. Head up the slope to come parallel with a wall on your right. Go on along a wide green trod with the wall now beside you on the right and the stream, in its deep ravine, on your left.

Join a farm access track, and where it turns sharp right go ahead towards a farm conversion. Pass through an unmarked gate, and before the first dwelling take a small gate on the left into a ginnel. Go through the next gate and down a long pasture to a gate into woodland. Descend the steep bumpy path, trees to your left and a wall to the right, to reach another gate. Walk through the yard of a house and onto the A646 where you turn left to stroll the short distance to the parking area.

# WALK 40

## *Hurstwood and Worsthorne Moor*

| | |
|---|---|
| **Distance** | 12km (7½ miles) |
| **Time** | 5 hours |
| **Terrain** | Many of the footpaths are in good repair and well waymarked; the unmarked path over Black Hameldon is in a very poor state and can be wet after rain |
| **Maps** | OS Explorer OL21 |

The tiny hamlet of Hurstwood nestles in a wooded hollow beneath the brooding moorland of Worsthorne. Charming Hurstwood Hall was built in Elizabethan times and beyond the hall, along a little lane, stands Spenser House, built about 1530. It is believed that the poet Edmund Spenser stayed there in 1579. When Hurstwood Reservoir was built in 1925 mixed woodland was planted to screen the dam from the village. Worsthorne Moor is one of the largest water-catchment areas in the south Pennines. Its development for supplying water to the then rapidly expanding town of Burnley began in earnest in the middle of the 19th century.

This is a strenuous, challenging walk for experienced and well-equipped ramblers.

Park in North West Water's car park, grid ref 882314. This is reached by a track leading to the right (west) of the phone box in the centre of Hurstwood. Go back to the entrance to the parking area and continue ahead for several steps before dropping down to the left over grass to a waymarked kissing gate. Walk the green trod that runs between small knolls, following it as it winds left and continues parallel with narrow, tree-lined Rock Water to your right. Ignore the arrowed way going off to the right and carry on along the bottom of the shallow grassy gorge. Pass through the kissing gate into

'Rockwater, part of the Forest of Burnley' and stroll on along the delightful way until it is blocked by a large projecting cliff. Then climb a narrow path to the left up the side of the gorge.

Stroll on along the continuing path along the rim of the gorge, steep slopes dropping to your right and a fenced pasture to your left. Go through the next kissing gate to leave Rockwater and continue to the next waymark.

Beyond, cross the footbridge over the stream and follow the white arrow that directs you slightly left rather than ahead. Walk along the crest of a little ridge towards a pylon. With the pylon and the fence to your left now, carry on along a narrow path marked occasionally by small, pillar-shaped cairns. Pass through a derelict wall

*Rock Water valley*

and go ahead to descend a small gully and then go over a stile. Stroll on to the next stile and continue along the little ridge, now with a huge area of rhododendrons on the hillside to your right and another large mass to your left – all very beautiful in June.

Continue on to join a reinforced track and turn right. Cross a footbridge and at the three-armed signpost turn left onto the Pennine Bridleway to walk below the magnificent spread of rhododendrons. Go over the stream on convenient stones and walk on along the main track. Where the track comes to a ford and a footbridge across the stream, do not cross, but leave the bridleway before both and walk ahead on a distinct path with a walled enclosure and then stone walling on your right, going on for a few metres. Continue on past more walling and then stride through the next walled enclosure. Just beyond, where the path divides, take the left fork and soon drop down to step across a little stream.

Climb straight up the slope to cross the track that covers a pipeline, just after it has disappeared under-ground, and go on ahead. After passing two small patches of bog continue straight up the steepish moorland beside a derelict wall on your right. As you climb the narrow but generally distinct path, look over the wall to see Cliviger Gorge. After 800 metres (½ mile) gentle climbing you reach the brow of the moor and then descend a short way, still beside the friendly wall, to a shallow valley where the wall turns away right.

Step across a wettish area through which a little stream runs and continue upwards on the now peaty path. For a short way the path continues up beside some old fence posts on the left, then moves away but remains parallel with the posts as they continue up the middle of a shallow wet gill to the left. At this point you reach a small, very wet area where the path disappears into ooze. Here you should take care to either walk along the soft rim of the little gill or wind round the far right side of the wet area. After negotiating this boggy patch remember to return to the path, which has now reappeared, and continue on up, aiming for more ancient posts.

Soon the path passes through carpets of bright green bilberry. Go past a few more ancient posts, and then on up a wide rough gully with rocks projecting through the peat, to come to a group of fissured gritstone boulders. Just above stands the trig point (479m (1580ft)) at Hoof Stones Height, where you may want to pause to enjoy the superb view.

Turn left to continue over Black Hameldon, a vast area of peat moorland. Keep to the middle of the ridge with the land dropping away slightly on both sides. Here there must once have been a good grassy trod, remnants of which you can still walk, but bad weather, boots and the tyres of

*Trig point at Hoof Stones Height*

various types of bicycles have spread erosion widely and today you need to pick your way carefully. Just after about 1.6km (1 mile) of this airy walking the way begins to descend through a deep, washed-out gully where the bedrock is exposed – here it is easier to walk down the left side of the sunken way. And then, as you near the valley, a green trod emerges and you can press on down.

Follow the green path as it swings steadily right to pass more fascinating boulders, Hare Stones, on their little hillock. Carry on winding right and climbing gently, then at a junction of several paths take the one to the right to join a wide track (Gorple Road). Here you turn left to make your return, although if you wish you can walk right for a short distance to sit below the Gorple Stones and enjoy the view of Gorple Upper Reservoir and a corner of Cant Clough reservoir.

If you have visited the Gorple Stones remember to turn right and continue on the sturdy track. Wind round Rams Clough, still high on the moor, and soon the great whaleback of Pendle Hill comes into view. Pass a commemorative seat, from where there is a pleasing view down towards Hurstwood, and at a gate and another seat Gorple Road carries on towards Worsthorne.

Here turn left and follow a good track that descends towards Hurstwood Reservoir. Turn right at the three-armed signpost to cross the footbridge and walk left to ascend a track. Continue on, ignoring the stile into the pine wood-land, and continue climbing to the top edge of the Scots pine plantation. Turn left to walk across pasture along the edge of the conifers to a stile into a delightful grassy walled track. Stroll along the way, which is shaded by beeches, and follow it where it turns left to go on to straddle a stile. Continue on down and then descend steps.

Turn left to carry on down the shady way and go through a kissing gate to cross a grassy clearing. Keep to the left side as directed by the waymarked posts and continue along a short grassy way between walls to arrive at a gate to the village and see the cluster of picturesque houses. Return to the phone box, cross the bridge over the stream and carry on to the car park.

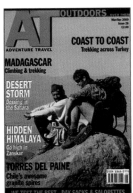

# LISTING OF CICERONE GUIDES

## NORTHERN ENGLAND

### LONG-DISTANCE TRAILS
The Dales Way
The Reiver's Way
The Alternative Coast to Coast
The Coast to Coast Walk
The Pennine Way
Hadrian's Wall Path
The Teesdale Way

### FOR COLLECTORS OF SUMMITS
The Relative Hills of Britain
Mts England & Wales Vol 2 – England
Mts England & Wales Vol 1 – Wales

### BRITISH CYCLE GUIDES
The Cumbria Cycle Way
Lands End to John O'Groats – Cycle
  Guide
On the Ruffstuff: 84 Bike Rides in
  North England
Rural Rides No.1 – West Surrey
Rural Rides No.2 – East Surrey
South Lakeland Cycle Rides
Border Country Cycle Routes
Lancashire Cycle Way

### CANOE GUIDES
Canoeist's Guide to the North-East

### LAKE DISTRICT AND
### MORECAMBE BAY
Coniston Copper Mines
Scrambles in the Lake District
More Scrambles in the Lake District
Walks in Silverdale and
  Arnside AONB
Short Walks in Lakeland 1 – South
Short Walks in Lakeland 2 – North
Short Walks in Lakeland 3 – West
The Tarns of Lakeland Vol 1 – West
The Tarns of Lakeland Vol 2 – East
The Cumbria Way &
  Allerdale Ramble
Winter Climbs in the Lake District
Roads and Tracks of the Lake District
The Lake District Angler's Guide
Rain or Shine – Walking in the
  Lake District
Rocky Rambler's Wild Walks
An Atlas of the English Lakes

### NORTH-WEST ENGLAND
Walker's Guide to the
  Lancaster Canal
Walking in Cheshire
Family Walks in the
  Forest Of Bowland
Walks in Ribble Country
Historic Walks in Cheshire
Walking in Lancashire
Walks in Lancashire Witch Country
The Ribble Way

### THE ISLE OF MAN
Walking on the Isle of Man
The Isle of Man Coastal Path

## PENNINES AND
## NORTH-EAST ENGLAND
Walks in the Yorkshire Dales – Vol 1
Walking in the South Pennines
Walking in the North Pennines
The Yorkshire Dales
Walks in the North York Moors –
  Vol 1
Walks in the North York Moors –
  Vol 2
Walking in the Wolds
Waterfall Walks – Teesdale and High
  Pennines
Walking in County Durham
Yorkshire Dales Angler's Guide
Backpacker's Britain – Northern
  England
Walks in Dales Country
Historic Walks in North Yorkshire
South Pennine Walks
Walking in Northumberland

### DERBYSHIRE, PEAK DISTRICT,
### EAST MIDLANDS
High Peak Walks
White Peak Walks Northern Dales
White Peak Walks Southern Dales
White Peak Way
The Viking Way
Star Family Walks Peak District &
  South Yorkshire
Walking In Peakland
Historic Walks in Derbyshire

### WALES AND WELSH BORDERS
Ascent of Snowdon
Welsh Winter Climbs
Hillwalking in Wales – Vol 1
Hillwalking in Wales – Vol 2
Scrambles in Snowdonia
Hillwalking in Snowdonia
The Ridges of Snowdonia
Hereford & the Wye Valley
Walking Offa's Dyke Path
The Brecon Beacons
Lleyn Peninsula Coastal Path
Anglesey Coast Walks
The Shropshire Way
Spirit Paths of Wales
Glyndwr's Way
The Pembrokeshire Coastal Path
Walking in Pembrokeshire
The Shropshire Hills – A Walker's
  Guide
Backpacker's Britain Vol 2 – Wales

### MIDLANDS
The Cotswold Way
West Midlands Rock
The Grand Union Canal Walk
Walking in Oxfordshire
Walking in Warwickshire
Walking in Worcestershire
Walking in Staffordshire
Heart of England Walks

## SOUTHERN ENGLAND
The Wealdway & the Vanguard Way
Exmoor & the Quantocks
Walking in the Chilterns
Walks in Kent Book 2
Two Moors Way
Walking in Dorset
Walking in Cornwall
A Walker's Guide to the Isle of Wight
Walking in Devon
Walking in Somerset
The Thames Path
Channel Island Walks
Walking in Buckinghamshire
The Isles of Scilly
Walking in Hampshire
Walking in Bedfordshire
The Lea Valley Walk
Walking in Berkshire
The Definitive Guide to
  Walking in London
The Greater Ridgeway
Walking on Dartmoor
The South West Coast Path
Walking in Sussex
The North Downs Way
The South Downs Way

## SCOTLAND
Scottish Glens 1 – Cairngorm Glens
Scottish Glens 2 – Atholl Glens
Scottish Glens 3 – Glens of Rannoch
Scottish Glens 4 – Glens of Trossach
Scottish Glens 5 – Glens of Argyll
Scottish Glens 6 – The Great Glen
Scottish Glens 7 – The Angus Glens
Scottish Glens 8 – Knoydart
  to Morvern
Scottish Glens 9 – The Glens
  of Ross-shire
Scrambles in Skye
The Island of Rhum
Torridon – A Walker's Guide
Ski Touring in Scotland
Walking the Galloway Hills
Walks from the West Highland
  Railway
Border Pubs & Inns –
  A Walker's Guide
Walks in the Lammermuirs
Scrambles in Lochaber
Walking in the Hebrides
Central Highlands: 6 Long
  Distance Walks
Walking in the Isle Of Arran
Walking in the Lowther Hills
North to the Cape
The Border Country –
  A Walker's Guide
Winter Climbs – Cairngorms
The Speyside Way
Winter Climbs – Ben Nevis &
  Glencoe
The Isle of Skye, A Walker's Guide

The West Highland Way
Scotland's Far North
Walking the Munros Vol 1 – Southern, Central
Walking the Munros Vol 2 – Northern & Cairngorms
Scotland's Far West
Walking in the Cairngorms

## IRELAND
The Mountains of Ireland
Irish Coastal Walks
The Irish Coast to Coast

## INTERNATIONAL CYCLE GUIDES
The Way of St James – Le Puy to Santiago cyclist's guide
The Danube Cycle Way
Cycle Tours in Spain
Cycling the River Loire – The Way of St Martin

## WALKING AND TREKKING IN THE ALPS
Grand Tour of Monte Rosa Vol 1
Grand Tour of Monte Rosa Vol 2
Walking in the Alps (all Alpine areas)
100 Hut Walks in the Alps
Chamonix to Zermatt
Tour of Mont Blanc
Alpine Ski Mountaineering Vol 1 Western Alps
Alpine Ski Mountaineering Vol 2 Eastern Alps
Snowshoeing: Techniques and Routes in the Western Alps
Alpine Points of View

## FRANCE, BELGIUM AND LUXEMBOURG
The Tour of the Queyras
Rock Climbs in the Verdon
RLS (Robert Louis Stevenson) Trail
Walks in Volcano Country
French Rock
Walking the French Gorges
Rock Climbs Belgium & Luxembourg
Tour of the Oisans: GR54
Walking in the Tarentaise and Beaufortain Alps
The Brittany Coastal Path
Walking in the Haute Savoie
Walking in the Ardennes
Tour of the Vanoise
Walking in the Languedoc
GR20 Corsica – The High Level Route
The Ecrins National Park
Walking the French Alps: GR5
Walking in the Cevennes
Vanoise Ski Touring
Walking in Provence
Walking on Corsica
Mont Blanc Walks
Walking in the Cathar region of south west France
Walking in the Dordogne

## PYRENEES AND FRANCE / SPAIN
Rock Climbs in the Pyrenees
Walks & Climbs in the Pyrenees

The GR10 Trail: Through the French Pyrenees
The Way of St James – Le Puy to the Pyrenees
The Way of St James – Pyrenees-Santiago-Finisterre
Through the Spanish Pyrenees GR11
The Pyrenees – World's Mountain Range Guide
The Pyrenean Haute Route
Walking in Andorra

## SPAIN AND PORTUGAL
Picos de Europa – Walks & Climbs
Andalusian Rock Climbs
The Mountains of Central Spain
Costa Blanca Rock
Walking in Mallorca
Rock Climbs in Majorca, Ibiza & Tenerife
Costa Blanca Walks Vol 1
Costa Blanca Walks Vol 2
Walking in Madeira
Via de la Plata (Seville To Santiago)
Walking in the Cordillera Cantabrica
Walking in the Canary Islands 1 West
Walking in the Canary Islands 2 East
Walking in the Sierra Nevada

## SWITZERLAND
The Jura: Walking the High Route & Ski Traverses
Walking in Ticino, Switzerland
Central Switzerland – A Walker's Guide
The Bernese Alps
Walking in the Valais
Alpine Pass Route
Walks in the Engadine, Switzerland

## GERMANY AND AUSTRIA
Klettersteig Scrambles in Northern Limestone Alps
King Ludwig Way
Walking in the Salzkammergut
Walking in the Black Forest
Walking in the Harz Mountains
Walking in the Bavarian Alps
Germany's Romantic Road
Mountain Walking in Austria
Walking the River Rhine Trail
Trekking in the Stubai Alps
Trekking in the Zillertal Alps

## SCANDINAVIA
Walking In Norway
The Pilgrim Road to Nidaros (St Olav's Way)

## EASTERN EUROPE
Trekking in the Caucausus
The High Tatras
The Mountains of Romania
Walking in Hungary

## CROATIA AND SLOVENIA
Walks in the Julian Alps
Walking in Croatia

## ITALY
Italian Rock

Walking in the Central Italian Alps
Central Apennines of Italy
Walking in Italy's Gran Paradiso
Long Distance Walks in Italy's Gran Paradiso
Walking in Sicily
Shorter Walks in the Dolomites
Treks in the Dolomites
Via Ferratas of the Italian Dolomites Vol 1
Via Ferratas of the Italian Dolomites Vol 2
Walking in the Dolomites
Walking in Tuscany
Trekking in the Apennines

## OTHER MEDITERRANEAN COUNTRIES
The Mountains of Greece
Climbs & Treks in the Ala Dag (Turkey)
The Mountains of Turkey
Treks & Climbs Wadi Rum, Jordan
Jordan – Walks, Treks, Caves etc.
Crete – The White Mountains
Walking in Palestine
Walking in Malta

## AFRICA
Climbing in the Moroccan Anti-Atlas
Trekking in the Atlas Mountains
Kilimanjaro

## NORTH AMERICA
The Grand Canyon & American South West
Walking in British Columbia
The John Muir Trail

## SOUTH AMERICA
Aconcagua

## HIMALAYAS – NEPAL, INDIA
Langtang, Gosainkund & Helambu: A Trekkers' Guide
Garhwal & Kumaon – A Trekkers' Guide
Kangchenjunga – A Trekkers' Guide
Manaslu – A Trekkers' Guide
Everest – A Trekkers' Guide
Annapurna – A Trekker's Guide
Bhutan – A Trekker's Guide DELAYED

## AUSTRALIA AND NEW ZEALAND
Classic Tramps in New Zealand

## TECHNIQUES AND EDUCATION
The Adventure Alternative
Rope Techniques
Snow & Ice Techniques
Mountain Weather
Beyond Adventure
The Hillwalker's Manual
The Book of the Bivvy
Outdoor Photography
The Hillwalker's Guide to Mountaineering
Map and Compass

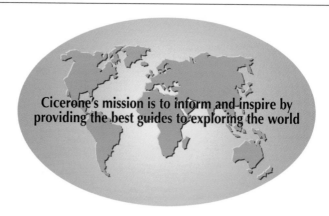

**Cicerone's mission is to inform and inspire by providing the best guides to exploring the world**

Since its foundation over 30 years ago, Cicerone has specialised in publishing guidebooks and has built a reputation for quality and reliability. It now publishes nearly 300 guides to the major destinations for outdoor enthusiasts, including Europe, UK and the rest of the world.

Written by leading and committed specialists, Cicerone guides are recognised as the most authoritative. They are full of information, maps and illustrations so that the user can plan and complete a successful and safe trip or expedition – be it a long face climb, a walk over Lakeland fells, an alpine traverse, a Himalayan trek or a ramble in the countryside.

With a thorough introduction to assist planning, clear diagrams, maps and colour photographs to illustrate the terrain and route, and accurate and detailed text, Cicerone guides are designed for ease of use and access to the information.

If the facts on the ground change, or there is any aspect of a guide that you think we can improve, we are always delighted to hear from you.

**Cicerone Press**
2 Police Square  Milnthorpe  Cumbria  LA7 7PY
Tel:01539 562 069   Fax:01539 563 417
e-mail:info@cicerone.co.uk   web:www.cicerone.co.uk